Kent Smugglers' Pubs

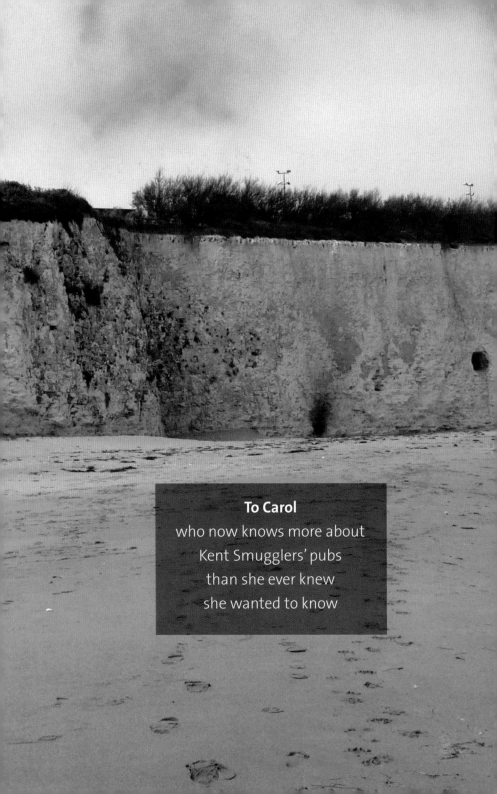

To Carol
who now knows more about
Kent Smugglers' pubs
than she ever knew
she wanted to know

Kent Smugglers' Pubs

Terry Townsend

First published in Great Britain in 2014
Reprinted 2015
Copyright © Terry Townsend 2014

British Library Cataloguing-in-Publication Data
A CIP record for this title is available from the
British Library

ISBN 978 0 85710 085 6

PiXZ Books
Halsgrove House, Ryelands Business Park,
Bagley Road, Wellington, Somerset TA21 9PZ
Tel: 01823 653777
Fax: 01823 216796
email: sales@halsgrove.com

An imprint of Halstar Ltd, part of the
Halsgrove group of companies
Information on all Halsgrove titles is
available at: www.halsgrove.com

Printed and bound in China by
Everbest Printing Co Ltd

CONTENTS

INTRODUCTION

By the year 1200, England had become the largest producer of the highest quality wool in the world. The raw product was eagerly sought by continental weavers and in 1203 King John imposed a tax on its export. Soon afterwards an import duty was imposed on wine, cloth and leather entering the country. From the moment these taxes were imposed they were evaded and so began the delicious deception of smuggling.

It is a common misconception that smuggling was confined to Cornwall. In practice, Kent's proximity to France established it as the main gateway for contraband. And, to the north west of the county, England's capital beckoned with its voracious market for all things illicit.

Kent also had a large number of suitable landing places all around the coast plus a legion of sailors, boat builders and

Kent had a large number of suitable contraband landing places all around the coast.

fishermen to provide the skilled men and vessels for the shipping. Inland people from every walk of life became involved in hiding, transporting and marketing contraband goods. Young and old, men and women, farmers, agricultural labourers and pub landlords all played their part.

Support for smuggling extended to churchmen, magistrates and the aristocracy who frequently connived in buying contraband, financing smuggling operations and protecting smugglers from the law.

As the centuries progressed, England became involved in a succession of foreign wars that required funding. New duties were imposed on a huge range of items that all became targets for smugglers. The illegal trade flourished because the majority of people did not consider it a crime. Indeed, at a time of widespread poverty in the rural south it provided a life-line for some and an opportunity to get back at an unjust and unfair society.

Smugglers trails were established where men and packhorses trekked through long nights under the weight of sacks of tea and barrels of spirits. All sorts of ingenious hiding places were made available along the routes in dugouts, stow-holds, barns, hayricks, coach houses, churches and the cellars and outbuildings of pubs.

Smuggling grew to massive proportions. It has been estimated that from 1700 to around 1850 a quarter of the country's import/export trade was illegal. The figure of the smuggler has provided material for innumerable fictional tales of intrigue and high adventure. In reality the law-makers had unwittingly created a climate in the country for the establishment of serious organised crime. The events which actually occurred in the heyday of smuggling provide us with stories every bit as wild as those that can be imagined.

THE SIGNAL

The pan of a flint-lock pistol was used to flash a warning. A lantern with a long funnel could pinpoint a light in a desired direction.

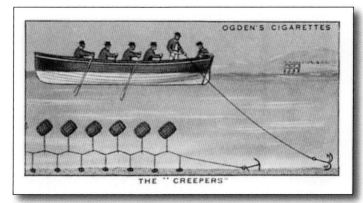

THE "CREEPERS"

All sorts of ingenious hiding places and practices were devised.

THE RIDING OFFICER

Riding Officers were generally ineffectual in combating smuggling.

Tangible links with this violent period are scarce, though there are some artifacts in a few museums. What has survived are the many authentic smuggling pubs. In most cases the local inn became the centre of operations for the smugglers, where plots were hatched, arrangements made and runs commissioned. The smugglers' pub served as a meeting place, recruitment centre, secret storage facility, distribution depot and valued customer.

Larger inns sometimes incorporated court houses; with gibbets and even gallows outside. Many pubs acted as temporary mortuaries and became emergency field hospitals where, after one of the numerous battles, injured smugglers and Revenue men were treated. Today these old buildings with their beamed low ceilings, high-backed settles, inglenook fireplaces, flagstone floors and secret hiding places are where you must go to get a feel or understanding for the desperate days of the free traders.

Legends and traditions about smuggling abound. Favourite stories of how the local community out-foxed customs officers have been repeated and embellished over centuries. Tales of hidden tunnels leading from one pub to another or from the pub to the church are still readily repeated. There is some evidence for a number of these claims but in reality smuggling became a brutal life and death game.

Through most of smuggling history free traders had it pretty much there own way. Preventative measures were poorly organized, understaffed and under funded. By the time of the Napoleonic Wars Kent had developed into a bloody battleground of civil unrest. Notorious smuggling gangs formed in a number of villages under charismatic fearless leaders. These men were able to muster horses, carts, pack-ponies and hundreds of helpers at short notice when a contraband run was imminent.

The crisis came to a head following the battle of Waterloo in 1815. The ending of the Napoleonic Wars brought the discharge – and therefore unemployment – of about 330,000 soldiers and sailors. This meant good recruiting opportunities for smuggling gangs but also a military force could now be made available to focus its attention on crushing the wicked trade.

In 1816 the Navy set up a 'coastal blockade' of armed sailors and marines on foot patrol. The smugglers' answer was to form in ever larger groups of 200 or more, protected by armed guards. The scene was set for some of the bloodiest conflicts.

Below left: Dragoons were sometimes called in to assist in chasing and apprehending smugglers.

Below right: Inland people from every walk of life became involved in hiding, transporting and marketing contraband goods.

THE DRAGOON

THE TUB MAN

11

Because smuggling became so entrenched throughout Kent, almost every pub at some time or another had an involvement. The collection featured here all have a documented association with smuggling. Wherever possible, I have chosen pubs that would still be recognizable to the 'gentlemen of the night' who frequented them all those years ago.

Today many pubs seem to change hands with monotonous regularity but even new landlords cannot change the stories behind the pubs themselves. In 1872 politician Sir William Harcourt observed: "As much of the history of England has been brought about in public houses as in the House of Commons." If you know where to look, and what to look for, a smugglers' pub will reward you with a wealth of history for free.

Ships like these of the East India company would hover offshore at Deal in the sheltered area of the Goodwin Sands called 'the Downs' so that Deal boatmen could buy tea and other contraband from them. The shallow draft Deal Lugger could negotiate the treacherous sanbanks where Revenue cutters and Navy blockade ships could not give chase.

Conyer
The Ship Inn

www.shipinnconyer.co.uk enquiries@shipinnconyer.co.uk 01795 520881

A left turn off the A2 at Teynham between Sittingbourne and Faversham leads to Conyer and The Ship Inn. Despite some modern housing development this is still a lovely, lonely spot hidden away in the middle of the marshes.

By the middle ages this former Roman hamlet had developed a strong smuggling community. The Saxon Shore Way is a link of smugglers' trails which follows the coastline through

This former baker's shop and black-smiths became a pub in 1802. It has recently been completely renovated and extended.

Above left: History student Georgia has made a study of Conyer's industries during the eighteenth and nineteenth century – smuggling being the foremost of them.

Above right: The courtyard and garden offer panoramic views of the creek, marina and Swale marshes.

here. A walk north along the creek easily shows how remote and suitable for running contraband the area would have been in the past.

Illicit goods landed at the creek would be carried inland; mixed with legitimate merchandise and sold in the market at Faversham. Larger hauls were transported to the London Turnpike, destined for the capital. Seized goods were taken under guard to the Faversham Customs House and later sold by auction.

As well as being a traditional local The Ship is also a quality gastro-inn.

On 22 March 1823 the following report appeared in the *Morning Post*: "In the night of Saturday last a considerable seizure was made near Conyer Creek, by the men belonging to the Preventative Service stationed at Elmly Ferry; the goods taken are French silks and other fancy articles, supposed to be of nearly £10,000 value; they have been deposited at the Custom-house, Faversham."

The building now occupied by the pub was originally a baker's shop dating to 1642 with a blacksmiths alongside. In 1802 it was owned by a Stephen Blaxland who successfully applied for an alehouse licence and called that part of the building The Ship. The other half continued as a bakery until 1831 when Sarah Beacon, a widow who had inherited the pub part, bought out the bakery and was granted a full licence for the house. In 1876 Sarah's son William sold the pub to aptly named brewer George Beer of the Star Brewery in Broad Street, Canterbury.

The Ship has recently been extended and very successfully renovated. It is light and airy with far reaching views across the creek, marina and marshes of the Swale. A gastro-restaurant is now the core of the business but The Ship still functions happily as a pub.

The pub is situated right on the creek and the Saxon Shore Way.

The Shipwright's Arms faces the creek so you have to enter from the car park shared with the boatyard.

Hollowshore
The Shipwright's Arms
www.theshipwrightsathollowshore.co.uk   01795 590088

As you enter this remote creek-side tavern your senses are greeted with a muted hubbub of conversation; a pleasant aroma of damp dogs, old timber, salt, tar and hoppy beer. First licensed in 1738, although much older than that, this ancient pub just oozes character.

As well as serving pirates and smugglers, the inn was a well known stopping place for Thames estuary sailors and fishermen. In those days it would have been quite normal for an inn serving mariners to provide them also with 'feminine comforts'.

Built of warm brick and clad in weatherboard The Shipwright's Arms has an interior akin to a small museum. Narrow doorways lead through to small low-beamed rooms packed with interesting artifacts and evocative photographs. The classic bars are full of nooks and crannies, original standing timbers, built-in settles, well-worn sofas in a relaxed no-frills but comfortable atmosphere.

If you want some ale... it had better be Goachers from the cask.

A number of items on display in the bar were recovered from the mud at low tide. These include a flintlock rifle and a Dutch cast-iron fireback of a type imported into England after the accession of William III in 1688. Dutch vessels would often sail the long way around the Isle of Sheppey to avoid detection. Contraband goods landed at Hollowshore were carried

Historical artifacts like this William III fireback continue to be revealed in the mud of the creek.

An eclectic mix of friendly characters make the pilgrimage to this remote pub.

17

On misty moonlit nights vast quantities of contraband were landed here.

up Faversham Creek on oyster boats and openly sold below the timber-framed Guildhall in the centre of the town.

Until recently The Shipwright's Arms was self-sufficient generating its own electricity. They still draw water from their own well and use propane gas for cooking. If you make it out here during the winter you can sit around one of the four open fires.

Adjacent to the pub is Testers Boatyard, which continues the centuries old tradition of wooden boat building. In 1860, the yard and the pub were owned by Thomas Madams. He paid £90 for the redundant prison hulk *Beresford*, which had been moored locally. After breaking it up he offered it for sale through an advertisement in the *Kentish Gazette* of October 9 which read: "Oak beams from 20 to 40 feet long, oak posts from 4 to 10 feet long, oak planks, fir beams, boards, doors, window frames &c., &c."

THE BEAR INN

This is the earliest surviving pub from the Middle Ages in Faversham....
The Bear Inn was purchased by Shepherd Neame in 1736 and originally included the buildings on either side of the pub.

Faversham
The Bear Inn

www.shepherdneame.co.uk/pubs/faversham/bear-inn 01795 532668

On Tuesdays, Fridays and Saturdays the tables and chairs outside The Bear in Faversham's historic Market Place, present an excellent people watching opportunity. The market is the oldest in Kent, going back at least 900 years and the setting is well-nigh perfect, with a backdrop of beautifully kept Tudor and Georgian buildings. For centuries contraband landed at Conyer Creek and Hollowshore was openly sold outside this ancient pub.

The light 'locals' front bar of The Bear is a late Victorian addition.

The origins of The Bear itself are lost in the mist of time. The best estimate is that the pub was probably present in the mid sixteenth-century when Henry VIII's fleet lay at anchor in Faversham Creek, but it may date from as early as 1272. The scene you see today from outside The Bear has changed so little it would still be recognised by Queen Elizabeth I, who visited the town in 1572 and by Shakespeare's touring company, who acted here in 1596.

The fascia on The Bear tells us that Shepherd Neame purchased the pub in 1736. This was at the time when oyster boats carried contraband up Faversham Creek. The town's expert smuggling sailors were not only of interest to the

Opposite: On Tuesdays, Fridays and Saturdays the tables and chairs outside The Bear in Faversham's historic Market Place, present an excellent people watching opportunity.

Licensees Chris and Marie Annand look cozy in the snug.

For centuries contraband landed at Conyer Creek and Hollowshore was openly sold outside The Bear. Faversham market is the oldest in Kent, going back at least 900 years.

In eighteenth-century Faversham experienced sailors were a constant target of Press Gangs.

HERE LIVED MICHAEL GREENWOOD, MARINER (1731/2 – 1812), WHO WAS PRESS – GANGED IN 1748, WRECKED OFF THE COAST OF MOROCCO IN 1768, AND THEN ENSLAVED BY THE MOORS FOR 17 MONTHS. AFTER BEING RANSOMED, HE RETURNED TO FAVERSHAM.

preventative men but also to the Royal Navy press gangs. One evening in 1748 oyster dredger Michael Greenwood was pressed in the market place – possibly after drinking in The Bear.

Ten years later he was serving in the battleship H.M.S. *Lichfield*, with a crew of about 350, when she was wrecked off the coast of North Africa. About half the crew survived and when they came ashore, were promptly enslaved by the Moors. During his captivity Greenwood kept a diary which is now in the possession of his descendants in Queensland, Australia. After seventeen months of negotiations a ransom secured the sailors' release and he returned to Faversham, settling in a sixteenth-century house at 89 Abbey Street, where he lived to be 80.

From 1736 until 1851 regular auctions of recovered contraband and smugglers' vessels were held at the nearby Custom House in Court Street. On 22 January 1823, during the time that Thomas Hammond was landlord of The Bear, the Customs House advertised for auction: "88 ¼ Gallons of BRANDY, 174 ½ ditto GIN, 2 pieces of FIR TIMBER, 451 HALF ANKERS, 4 ANCHORS, two WARPS. 54 FIR OARS."

This half-timbered, jetted house with its diamond paned latticed windows was home to mariner Michael Greenwood who was press ganged outside The Bear in 1748.

Today there is a relaxed atmosphere in this three room pub. Walking down the side corridor which connects the rooms is like walking back in history. The light 'locals' front bar is late Victorian, then there's an older snug in the middle. The dining/saloon bar at the rear is the sixteenth-century part of the building. The serving bar, with an interesting frieze, also runs down the length of the pub connecting the three rooms.

Walking down the side corridor which connects the rooms is like walking back in history.

Faversham
The Anchor Pub & Restaurant
www.anchor-pub.co.uk info@anchor-pub.co.uk 01795 536471

A plaque on the Anchor Inn at 52 Abbey Street reads: "This ancient tavern, formerly The Anchor and Standard has offered hospitality for at least 300 years." The pub was probably present by 1695 and the address was earlier given as Standard Quay. Today Abbey Street is recognized as one of Britain's finest mediaeval streets. It was laid out as an impressive roadway to the Royal Abbey founded in 1147 by King Stephen and his wife Queen Matilda.

The brown ship-lap boarded annex on the left is the coffee shop area.

The presence of an old piano adds to the comfy, pubby atmosphere of the bar.

The town's famous brewing tradition dates back to this time when the Cluniac monks discovered that Faversham's pure spring water could be combined with locally-grown malting barley to produce particularly fine ale. John Caslock, who was the last Abbot of Faversham, was exporting beer through the town's creek in 1525. Through the centuries, the two main commodities being smuggled out of Faversham's bustling

The old inglenook is redolent of clay pipes and sea shanties.

port were wool and beer! In 1699 there were 24 breweries in the town.

When Daniel Defoe came here in 1724 the majority of the houses along Abbey Street and Court Street were likely to have been taverns or brothels. Writing about the massive explosion that had occurred at the Gunpowder Mill a few years earlier he said:

"I know nothing else this town is remarkable for, except the most notorious smuggling trade, carry'd on partly by the assistance of the Dutch, in their oyster-boats, and partly by other arts, in which they say, the people hereabouts are arriv'd to such a proficiency, that they are grown monstrous rich by that wicked trade; nay, even the owling trade (so they call the clandestine exporting of wool) has seem'd to be transposed

Tons of contraband was landed here on Faversham quay alongside legitimate cargoes.

The Customs House in Court Street where seized contraband was auctioned.

from Rumney Marsh to this coast, and a great deal of it had been carry'd on between the mouth of the East-Swale and the North-Foreland."

Faversham Custom House was established in Court Street where Revenue officers were based. They patrolled an extensive area from Milton to Whitstable, Herne Bay and Reculver. Huge quantities of seized contraband was stored at the Customs House and later auctioned off here. Pigot's *Directory* informs us that Jesse Buesden was in charge of The Anchor from 1824 through 1840. The list of goods auctioned during Jessie's time makes interesting reading. For example:

On 3 February 1824 cloth, cambrick, nankeen and 81 yards of paper hangings and, on 26 March in the same year 150 galls Brandy and 108 galls Geneva. Brandy and Gin was again for sale; on 17 January 1826 and on 17 March *The Nancy*, a 93 ton smack plus 2 boats, brandy and gin etc. There can hardly have been a day during the first 250 years of its existence when smuggling was not discussed or planned over a mug of Faversham ale under the roof of this ancient creek side inn.

This character pub has been tastefully refurbished to retain the ancient hallmarks of the original inn. The large two-bar pub-restaurant has traditional pine boards and a brick floor with an enormous inglenook at one end and a huge wood-burner in the opposite room. The brown ship-lap boarded annex is the coffee shop area and the family-friendly establishment also has a large beer garden ideal for summer afternoons.

NORTH COAST & FORELAND

Seasalter
The Oyster Pearl Pub & Restaurant

www.oysterpearlrestaurant.vpweb.co.uk/default.html
oysterpearlrestaurant@hotmail.com 01227 272705

During the eighteenth century the coast at Seasalter was an ideal spot for landing contraband. The beach consists of mud and shingle, so there was little risk of damage in beaching vessels, and open marshland backed onto the shore. The nearby Forest of Blean provided plenty of cover for the landed goods.

The contraband was brought ashore close to the Blue Anchor pub (recently renamed The Oyster Pearl) and passed on through a network of farms near the coast whose buildings benefited from cunningly-concealed compartments, windowless rooms, and secret shafts. The next stage was to move the contraband inland to Blue House Farm situated in a remote

The former Blue Anchor, now The Oyster Pearl pub restaurant is today surrounded by caravan holiday parks.

The ultra modern interior gives no clue to its smuggling history.

This early photograph shows the land behind the Blue Anchor as the smugglers would have known it.

location outside of Lenham. Here heavy carts were loaded with the brandy and tobacco for onward shipment along the turnpike to the major markets in London.

This private house in Genesta Avenue (nearly opposite the more modern 'Rose in Bloom' pub) was for decades the headquarters of the Seasalter Company.

The whole enterprise was highly organized and administered by a federation of ostensibly very respectable individuals operating under the innocent collective title of 'The Seasalter Company'. The Founder member was Dr Isaac Rutton of Ashford, who leased Seasalter Parsonage Farm in 1740 and used it as his headquarters.

It is now a private house in Genesta Avenue, nearly opposite the more modern Rose in Bloom pub. Rumours of smugglers' tunnels were confirmed a couple of years ago when part of the back garden of Seasalter Parsonage Farm collapsed.

A letter exists, written by the corrupt Reverend Thomas Patten who was vicar of Seasalter from 1711 to 1764 and who operated as a double agent informer. He lived in the vicarage which stood about 200 yards from The Blue Anchor.

The letter, dated 12 March 1746, was written from Canterbury and gives a clue to the size of the gangs employed. Also how pitifully inadequate the forces of law and order were, to combat the brazen activities of such large numbers of violent men:

"On the 7th instant, a gang of about one hundred and fifty smugglers landed their cargo… and went from the sea coast about 9.0a.m. Sixty three men and from eighty to ninety horses went by Whitstable and Faversham, and the rest went over Grove Ferry."

The Seasalter Company flourished for over a century from 1740, and must have made many fortunes for its partners. Certainly one man, William Baldock, benefited to an unprecedented degree: when he died in 1812, he left over a million pounds – more than £200 million in today's money.

The Oyster Pearl, which stands near the point where the Faversham Road turns west to follow the sea wall along the Swale coast, is now much more of a restaurant than a pub. The ultra modern interior gives no clue to its smuggling history. Today the spot is surrounded by caravan holiday parks.

The ideal contraband landing beaches seen from the car park of the nearby 'Rose in Bloom' pub.

The wonky Old Neptune Inn, standing directly on the beach with no sea defences has more than once been knocked down in violent storms and re-built using the same timbers.

Whitstable
Old Neptune
www.neppy.co.uk   01227 272262

During the final decades of the eighteenth century the local newspapers in Whitstable carried regular reports of huge contraband seizures by the authorities. In the year 1788/9 no fewer than thirteen such significant seizures of goods and vessels were reported.

At this time the town had 52 pubs and a number of them (some next door to each other) stood either side of the narrow street called 'Island Wall' which was the centre of smuggling activities. Several of these properties are now private houses but still retain the original pub names including: The King's Head (No. 18), The Guinea (No. 31) and the Fisherman's Arms (No. 34). Between Island Wall and the sea, built right on the beach is the wonky 'Old Neptune Inn'.

The inn you see today is not actually as 'Old' as it appears – although the fabric is. The building has been knocked down in tempestuous storms and re-built several times over the years often incorporating original timbers. The warped and twisted timber structure, with its old wooden foundations, seems to accommodate movement. This can be seen in the angle of the window frames and experienced when walking across the sloping floor trying not to spill your pint.

The fact that Whitstable played a full and active part in the free-trade is unsurprising, but what makes the town more unusual is its involvement in a lucrative and successful variation of the activities – the trade in smuggled prisoners of war. Between the Napoleonic War years of 1793 and 1814 enormous numbers of French POWs were brought to England,

The warped and twisted timber structure seems to accommodate movement as can be seen in the angle of the floors and door frames. The interior is cozy even when it is blowing a gale outside.

Island Wall was the centre of smuggling activities. Several of these properties still retain the original pub names.

putting a considerable strain on the country's resources and leading to a vast prison building programme which included Dartmoor.

Many French prisoners lived in appalling conditions in filthy, overcrowded prisons and prison hulks. Relatives of the wealthier prisoners were willing to pay handsomely for their safe return. Through an elaborate network of contacts and safe havens, those who succeeded in escaping would first be brought to London. From the capital they were smuggled to Whitstable on a hoy or oyster boat before being given safe passage home to France.

The Fisherman's Arms is one of the many former pubs in this old quarter of the town.

However, this period was exceptional, and smuggling in Whitstable generally followed the national pattern, with smugglers moving the familiar cargoes of brandy, tobacco, lace and gin, using bribery and violence.

This unpretentious weather-boarded old tavern can get very busy in the summer. It has plenty of quirky bits and pieces decorating the bar and rooms. If you don't mind your pubs being a bit scruffy, as long as they are friendly, this is for you.

Herne Bay
The Ship

www.theshiphernebay.com 01227 366636

On Easter Monday 20 April 1821 members of the North Kent Gang of smugglers rendezvoused at the home of John Richardson at Hoath, 3 miles south east, inland of Herne Bay. Here pistols, blunderbusses and clubs (or bats) were distributed to the twenty or so men who were to form the protection guard. A further forty men were to undertake the unloading and transportation.

Working to a pre-arranged plan devised by James West the smugglers split into a number of smaller groups and made their way by different routes to meet up by The Ship Inn. Proceeding down the beach, the fighting men fanned out in the usual style and the tub men settled down to await the arrival of the boat carrying the contraband. The night was wet and dark. About 2.45 a.m. the vessel's lights winked in answer to the signals from the beach and everything appeared to be going as planned.

Unknown to West and his men a blockade party consisting of Midshipman Sydenham Snow, Quartermaster David North

The Ship is said to to be the oldest building in Herne Bay.

OGDEN'S CIGARETTES

THE MIDSHIPMAN

Midshipmen like Sydenham Snow were paid only £36 a year but were willing to put their life on the line to discharge their duty.

and Seamen Wilson and Barker had put ashore shortly before and were proceeding on a routine patrol along the beach in the direction of the gang. Alerted by the noise of the cargo being run ashore, Snow drew his pistol and challenged the smugglers in the King's name.

Undeterred by the fusilade of shots in reply the young Midshipman pressed forward but his own pistol misfired. He drew his knife and charged but was almost immediately brought down; wounded in the shoulder and in the leg. His companions were kept at bay by the firing, unable to offer any immediate assistance.

With the landing completed the smugglers made off and Snow's companions attended their wounded comrade and carried him into The Ship Inn which stood only a few yards away. He was treated by a Naval surgeon from Birchington but died the following day, complaining to a comrade that it was his regret: "That his life had not been yielded in open battle with the enemies of his

The successful refurbishment of the old inn reflects a nautical theme. There are uninterrupted sea views from the bars and restaurant.

Ship Inn, Herne Bay

The Ship when Herne Bay was in its heyday as a seaside resort after the construction of the promenade and pier.

A poster on the promenade in front of The Ship details the story of the smuggling era.

E SHIP INN

dating from the late seventeenth century, is set in the heart of Herne , where the road from Canterbury reached the sea. Here were the Herne Bay (or Hearn Bay) as a coastal resort.

ded extension to The Ship was added around 1800 as a for the military from the nearby battery of guns ers. They were based on the Downs, (where stands today) to defend the coast against the Napoleonic Wars. The upper room was used as a coroner's court.

Local coastal vessels (known as hoys) which carried cargo, and occasionally passengers, anchored opposite and unloaded onto the beach. Midshipman Sydenham Snow, of the Coastal Blockade Service, was shot here on April 21st 1821 when he came upon a group of men loading smuggled goods onto their cart. He attempted to shoot first but his pistol failed; the smugglers fired with their muskets. Badly injured, Snow was taken to the Ship. He died three days later and is buried at Herne. No one was found guilty of the crime.

Customers enjoying the view from the newly built sun-trap terrace are protected from the wind by large glass screens.

country instead of being sacrificed in a vile midnight encounter with a gang of outlaws".

For 500 years the white painted Ship Inn stood here on the beach, serving the local fishing and smuggling community, before a group of Victorian investors from London built a pleasure pier and the promenade on which it now enjoys a central position. It is thought to be the oldest building in Herne Bay dating to around 1385. The weatherboarded extension was added around 1800 and used by military personnel from gun batteries based nearby during the period of the Napoleonic Wars.

Following a period of closure The Ship has now been completely refurbished and it re-opened in February 2010. Also in 2010 an outside decking area was added so that diners and drinkers can sit outside in a sheltered area enjoying uninterrupted sea views.

Herne Bay
The Smugglers Inn

www.shepherdneame.co.uk/pubs/herne-bay/smugglers-inn 01227 741395

The Smugglers Inn stands in the centre of the village of Herne on a spot traditionally known as Smuggler's Corner, at the junction of Herne Street and School Lane. The building adjoins a curved terrace of half timbered smugglers' cottages and is across the road from the beautiful twelfth-century St Martin of Tours church in whose graveyard smugglers and the brave Blockade Midshipman Sydenham Snow are buried.

The specially constructed lookout window next to the chimney used by the North Kent Gang.

On the evening of 20 April 1821 members of the North Kent Gang were reported as having spent a considerable amount of time at the inn. They were somewhat the worse for wear when they left to make their way to a planned landing at Herne Bay. Midshipman Snow, on patrol with three other

The imposing Victorian façade of The Smugglers Inn.

The Smugglers Inn is a good, all-round village local with bar, lounge and real fire.

Captain James William McCulloch (known to his men as Flogging Joey) attended the military funeral of Midshipman Snow.

blockade men, challenged the smugglers on the beach outside the Ship Inn and paid for it with his life.

The main road from Canterbury to Herne Bay curves round the eastern end of the churchyard. This lovely church has distinctive alternate bands of flint and Kentish ragstone at the base of the tower. It is here, on the western side, that Snow's headstone can be found – although it looks to have been moved from its original position.

The headstone of Midshipman Snow on the western side at the foot of the church tower.

Snow was laid to rest in the churchyard here on 30 April with full military honours. His commanding officer, Captain James William McCulloch (known to his men as Flogging Joey) and other officers from H.M.S. *Severn* followed his coffin. The gunfire of the salute was heard in the pub while smugglers from the cottages opposite looked on.

A little further up the hill from Smuggler's Corner, set back on the left, is a building known as Box Iron House, from its original shape. When water mains were laid here in 1907, workmen came upon a honeycomb of arched cellars, approached by an interior staircase. A passage led out to the side of the road, where there was a trapdoor and chains for lowering barrels. Cellars were also discovered under the roadway itself.

A view of the pub from the churchyard in former days when it was called the Prince Albert.

41

The curved terrace of half timbered smugglers' cottages adjoins the inn.

When water mains were laid under Box Iron House in 1907, workmen came upon a honeycomb of arched cellars, approached by an interior staircase.

Today The Smugglers Inn has a clean minimalist air. Darts and Pool trophies have replaced the wealth of maritime exhibits that adorned the bar forty years ago. In the 1960s a store of old contraband spirit bottles was found in a hiding place behind a wall in the cellar. This chance discovery led to a more careful search which revealed a crypt-like recess in the cellar in which a number of casks, containing rum of extreme potency, were literally unearthed.

The Smugglers Inn is a good, all-round village local with bar, lounge and real fire. It has a pleasant lawned area of garden to the rear with an awning shelter and decking with tables and chairs and sun umbrellas.

Kingsgate
Captain Digby

www.captaindigby.co.uk 01843 867764

In 1769, on the sands below the Captain Digby, Revenue men ambushed the much-fabled Broadstairs smuggler Joss Snelling and his notorious 'Callis Court Gang' when they were caught in the act of landing illicit cargo. The bloody fracas that ensued here has gone down in history as 'The Battle of Botany Bay'.

Round the southern headland is Kent's best surfing beach which is commemorated as Joss Bay. In the confusion of the battle, Snelling and four accomplices escaped through an opening in the cliffs. A courageous but unfortunate Riding Officer accosted them at the cliff-top, but they shot him and fled. He was carried to the Captain Digby Inn, where he died.

Before cliff-face erosion the hole (seen on the right) was the entrance to a smugglers' tunnel which emerged at beach level.

On that day, fifteen of Snelling's men also died. Some others who were captured were subsequently hanged at Gallows Field in Sandwich. The gang leader himself managed to

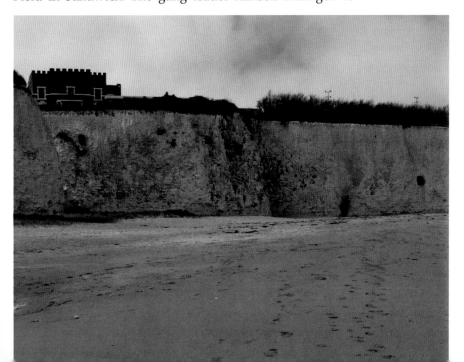

The present Captain Digby inn was developed from the stable block of the original.

Below right: The Captain Digby has a small bar area but functions mainly as an extensive family eatery.

Below: Following the 1769 battle, Revenue men found two dead smugglers and one mortally wounded in Rosemary Cottage.

Bottom: The hole in the wall of Rosemary Cottage made by an unexploded shell fired from a German Battleship anchored in the bay.

escape; he had a happy knack over the years of slipping through the net. Despite the dangerous nature of his profession he managed to live for an incredible 96 years.

The Captain Digby inn we see today has been developed from the stable block of the original which disappeared when part of the cliff collapsed in a severe storm in October 1816. Much more a restaurant than a pub, the Digby has a bar area but functions mainly as an extensive family eatery.

The inn was built by Lord Holland between 1763 and 1768 as a 'Bede House' – a place for drinking and entertainment of his guests. It is named after his nephew Robert who commanded a warship of the English fleet in 1759.

Joss Snelling lived in the adjacent village of Reading Street, where there is still plenty of evidence of the smuggling days. In 1954 contraband storage caves were revealed in the garden of a house in Elmwood Avenue when it collapsed under the weight of a bulldozer. Following the 1769 battle Revenue men mounted a search and found two dead smugglers and one mortally wounded, in Rosemary Cottage in the village street.

At a junction with Callis Court Road is Fig Tree Road. Along on the right, the house with a small copper cupola, was the 'Fig Tree Inn' and anyone seeking work as a smuggler could find it here. In 1784 the landlord eavesdropped on a conversation between officers of the 13th Light Dragoons quartered nearby and heard they were planning a raid on Deal. He sent notice by carrier pigeon to his brother who ran the Drum at Walmer (gone). Consequently, a force of 300 smugglers turned out to prevent the troops riding into the town.

Top: This house in Lanthorn Road was originally the dairy to Callis Court Farm and was the home of the notorious smuggler Joss Snelling.

Above: The former 'Fig Tree Inn' where anyone seeking work as a smuggler could find it.

Former contraband storage caves in the collapsed garden of a house in Elmwood Avenue.

Broadstairs
Tartar Frigate & Seafood Restaurant
www.tartarfrigate.co.uk 01843 862013

Broadstairs was originally known by the Anglo-Saxon name of 'Bradstowe' which means 'Broad Place'. The name evolved into Broadstairs as a result of the broad 'Chapel Stairs' which once led up from the beach to St Mary's chapel.

Visiting the area in 1723, Daniel Defoe wrote: "Bradstow is a small fishing hamlet of some 300 souls, of which 27 follow the occupation of fishing, the rest would seem to have no visible means of support! I am told that the area is a hot bed of smuggling. When I asked if this was so, the locals did give me the notion that if I persisted in this line of enquiry some serious injury might befall my person."

The castellated Fort House (re-named Bleak House) where Dickens stayed for a number of extended summer holidays.

The eighteenth-century flint-built pub/restaurant is located at the bottom of Harbour Street.

Over a century later Charles Dickens came to a similar conclusion about the inactivity of the fishermen. In 'Our English Watering Place' from *Reprinted Pieces* he wrote: "Looking at them, you would say that surely these must be the laziest boatmen in the world… Whether talking about shipping in the channel, or gruffly unbending over mugs of beer at the public-house, you would consider them the slowest men. The chances are you might stay here for ten seasons, and never see a boatman in a hurry."

Dickens did indeed stay, on and off, for many seasons from 1837 through to 1851. During his first visit smuggling gang leader Joss Snelling was still alive. Eight years earlier Snelling had inexplicably been presented to the future Queen Victoria; introduced as 'the famous Broadstairs smuggler'. He died peacefully at the age of ninety-six in October 1837 but the smuggling tradition continued with his son, George, and his grandson.

It seems more than likely that Dickens bought some supplies from the smugglers but he also seems to have had a little

47

Seafaring themes decorate the bar and dining room.

unease. On 17 August 1850, his pregnant wife Catherine was confined in London. He was staying in Fort House, Broadstairs and complained to her in a letter that the Preventative men were disturbing his muse: "I have arranged to write in the Drawing Room. I tried Georgina's room, but the Preventative men looked at me, and you know what a settler that would be to the most retiring of writers."

There is a renowned seafood restaurant upstairs with wonderful views over the bay.

'The Goblins Who Stole a Sexton' is the title of one of Dickens's Christmas stories, published with his *Pickwick Papers*. It features Gabriel Grub, a mean-hearted church sexton who is digging a grave on Christmas Eve when he is surprised by a host of goblins led by a goblin king. Grub is quizzed about the smuggled Dutch gin 'Hollands' he has been drinking:

'"What have you got in that bottle?" said the goblin. "Hollands, sir" replied the sexton, trembling more than ever; for he had bought it off the smugglers, and he thought that perhaps his questioner might be in the excise department of the goblins'.

Dickens also visited the 'Tartar Frigate' during his stays and described it as: "the coziest little sailor's inn that is to be met around the coast... the very walls have long ago learned 'Tom Bowling' and 'The Bay of Biscay' by heart and would be thankful for a fresh song."

Located practically on the beach at the bottom of Harbour Street, The Tartar Frigate takes it's name from the H.M.S. *Tartar*, a Naval ship built in the local shipyard. There has been a pub on this site since Elizabethan times but the present building dates from the eighteenth century.

The flint-built pub/restaurant occupies an idyllic position overlooking the harbour and the bay and has been the haunt of smugglers, customs men and seafarers for more than 300 years. Seafaring themes decorate the bar and dining room and there is a great seafood restaurant upstairs.

The old Harbour Master's House stands opposite the pub.

Pegwell Bay
The Belle Vue Tavern

www.thebellevuetavern.co.uk/Home   info@thebellevuetavern.co.uk
01843 593991

In the cliffs below The Belle Vue Tavern is a small opening about 8ft above the level of the beach. This leads to 500ft of low, artificial excavations. It is called Frank Illingworth's Tunnel after the man who explored and wrote about it in 1938.

The smugglers' tunnel slopes slightly towards the sea and, before the cliff face eroded, would have emerged at beach level. During his exploration, Illingworth discovered an ancient pistol and 3 buttons from an Exciseman's tunic. Other tunnels connected the inn with the eighteenth-century cottages across the road.

The delightful Belle Vue Tavern dates back to at least 1760.

Pegwell Bay on a moonlit night was the perfect landing place for the free traders' contraband. The village blacksmith, known simply as 'Big Jim' ran the local smuggling gang. The luxury illegal goods were cached in the cellars of the tavern where they could be quickly removed in an emergency to the safe houses across the way.

The cliff top Belle Vue is a delightful pub with extensive views. Now owned by Shepherd Neame it was formerly a Tompson & Wotton house. It dates back to at least 1760, and in all probability, was offering accommodation, refreshment and stabling from as early as 1720.

By the beginning of the nineteenth century the inn had cleaned up its smuggling image and was receiving the patronage of royalty. In 1830 the Duchess of Kent and her daughter Princess Victoria visited the pub and its renowned tea gardens. They must have enjoyed the local shrimps served up by the then host John Cramp, for he was to receive the royal appointment as 'Purveyor of Essence of Shrimps in ordinary to Her Majesty the Queen'

Among the many other celebrity visitors, Charles Dickens called with his family while on holiday in nearby Broadstairs, commenting: "The shrimps were delightful, the ale better." He also introduced children's writer Hans Christian Andersen to the delights of The Belle Vue when they visited Pegwell in 1842.

Illegal goods were cached in the tavern cellars and, in an emergency, quickly removed to cottages across the way.

The terrace garden enjoys some of the best sea views to be found in Kent.

Tunnels in the cliff led up to the inn and connected with the eighteenth century cottages across the road.

The Belle Vue was completely refurbished in early 2010 to become a well presented pub with a contemporary restaurant. Although just a stone's-throw from the busy centre of Ramsgate, it is a haven of peace and tranquillity enjoying some of the best sea views to be found in Kent.

CHANNEL PORTS

Sandwich
The King's Arms Hotel

www.kingsarms-sandwich.co.uk/index.htm   01304 617330

The Royal Coat of Arms is that of Elizabeth I who visited Sandwich in 1573 and stayed opposite in the King's Lodgings.

Today Sandwich is about two miles from the sea, but at one time large warships and trading vessels were able to sail up the River Stour to 'Sandwich Haven' harbour. The beach at Sandwich Bay was a favourite place for landing illicit cargoes and, in 1817, Blockade men discovered a wood-lined contraband store pit here. This was one of a number of similar cleverly contrived hiding places concealed by a thick layer of shingle to defeat the use of probes.

The King's Arms stands on the corner of Church Street and Strand Street which reputedly has more old timbered houses than any other street in England.

In general, rivalry did not exist between smuggling gangs. They were prepared to work together for mutual benefit but something went wrong here in Sandwich in 1746. Almost 12 tons of tea was being landed by a joint force of the Hawkhurst Gang and another band from Wingham. Before the landing was complete the Wingham men fled the scene with their share of the cargo. Incensed by this action, the ruthless Hawkhurst men gave chase brandishing their swords. In the ensuing battle seven of the Wingham men were wounded and the victors gained forty horses and most of the tea.

The massive corner post, dated 1592, is carved into a grotesque devil crouched upon its haunches. This was one of the last earthly things condemned prisoners saw!

The King's Arms stands on the corner of Church Street and Strand Street which is said to have more old timbered houses than any other street in England. The inn is early Tudor and was first recorded as the Queens Arms, marking a visit to the town by Elizabeth I. in 1573. It was in 1687, during the reign of James II, that the inn changed its name to the King's Arms.

Gallows Field today is part of a nature reserve established in 1970.

Gallows Field, further down Strand Street, represents the gruesome side of historic Sandwich. From the old gaol in St Peter's Street, prisoners were transported along the Strand past the King's Arms on their way to be hanged. There would have been great excitement here on the days of public executions. In 1803 people poured out of the inn and followed the procession to Gallows Field to witness the execution of eight

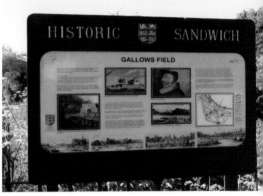

of Joss Snelling's smuggling gang who had been captured at Kingsgate following the 'Battle of Botany Bay'.

Through the 1700s and into the 1800s the inn was a well known coaching house. Drivers and guards, acting as look-outs and informers were in the pay of smugglers from Wrotham in West Kent. The Wrotham Gang could muster large numbers of horses and specialised in transporting contraband from Sandwich through Wrotham to London.

Today at the King's Arms there is an emphasis on the accommodation and restaurant side of the business but you can still pop in for a pint. The internal appearance is just as appealing as the outside. A particular feature is the original open fire-place in the bar lounge area as you walk in.

Above left: The King's Arms Hotel boasts that it provides the attention to detail, flexibility and standards often sought, but rarely found.

Above right: Further along Strand Street from the pub is the former place of public execution.

The bar is always decorated with Kentish hops.

Graham Stiles, pictured behind the bar, became mine host in 1980 and continues to run the pub with his wife and son.

Deal
The King's Head & Channel View Guest House

www.kingsheaddeal.co.uk/index.html bookings@kingsheaddeal.co.uk
01304 368194

For a while, during the seventeenth and eighteenth centuries, the small fishing town of Deal grew to become the busiest port in England and the foremost smuggling town in the world. Ownership of the boats used for smuggling was dominated by the landlords of the seafront inns who financed the illicit trade. Every pub was a smugglers' pub.

Although never strictly a gang, the boatmen of Deal became legendary for their seamanship and for their shallow draft luggers and 40ft long galleys that held as many as 30 oarsmen. With the occasional additional boost from a small sail they could make the trip across to France in less than five hours.

Until very recently miles of Deal beach resembled an untidy boatyard covered in oil, with old frame mounted diesel engines and hawsers to pull the vessels ashore. It's tidy now but I miss the old scene.

The King's Head is rightly famous for its award winning floral displays that adorn the front of the building throughout summer.

The tiny cellar is accessed from inside the bar. The restricted space suggests it may be a small remnant of what was once a much larger storage area.

This handsome three storey Georgian inn stands just across the road from the promenade and shares its seafront terrace with the Port Arms.

Always central to the smuggling action was The King's Head. This handsome three storey Georgian inn stands just across the road from the promenade and shares its seafront terrace with the Port Arms. Richard Dawes was the landlord at The King's Head on Thursday 15 January, 1784, when the beach here was the scene of the blackest day for the townsfolk of Deal.

The Three Compasses restaurant was formerly a pub with a smuggling run at the top of the building allowing contraband to be spirited away through linking attics and across the rooftops of neighbouring buildings.

As a result of the carrier pigeon warning from the landlord of the Fig Tree Inn (see Kingsgate) 300 people were prepared and able to repel a raid by the 13th Light Dragoons from Sandwich. However, on the following day, the Dragoons were reinforced by the 38th Foot who had force marched from Canterbury.

There had been severe storms for sometime prior to this and all the Deal boats were pulled well up on the beach. Acting

Today the pub has a wealth of interesting maritime items displayed in the comfortable dimly lit areas around a central servery.

on the direct orders of the then Prime Minister, William Pitt the Younger, the troops moved down to the beach smashing and setting fire to the whole fleet of fishing boats and luggers. As a result of this draconian action a number of fishermens' families ended up in the workhouse.

The burning of the boats gave the Government forces only temporary relief from the activities in Deal. Soon it was business as usual. In 1801, when Richard Dawes was landlord of The King's Head, smugglers had no trouble enlisting the help of local residents when the Revenue men forced a smuggling lugger onto the town beach. The mob attacked the luckless preventives, and brought ashore the cargo of tobacco, playing cards and bolts of fine cloth.

The first mention of The King's Head Tavern was in 1643 in relation to nearby properties.

Today the pub has a wealth of interesting maritime items displayed in the comfortable dimly lit areas around a central servery. Steps lead down directly from the bar to the cellar where contraband would have been stored.

The totally unspoilt Ship Inn is tucked away behind the seafront in Middle Street. The first reference to a building on this site was in 1694.

Deal
Ship Inn
01304 372222

This totally unspoilt pub is tucked away behind the seafront in Middle Street, in the very old maritime part of Deal. The interior is timeless and charmingly authentic, having retained much of its historic nautical fascination. You don't need a great deal of imagination to picture the smuggling boatmen of Deal swapping stories or singing sea shanties in the cosy back bar.

The Ship Inn today is a tranquil haven – but it wasn't ever so. In the early 1800s, after the wars with France were finally over, smuggling soared to new heights. Deal had already become the country's most notorious centre for the illicit trade and now there was a surplus of demobilized sailors moving into the town seeking profitable peacetime employment. In 1812 the pub was acquired by a retired Naval Sea Captain called David Ross.

During this time Revenue men faced constant danger in the town and were killed during skirmishes. Middle Street became a lawless no-go area. In its determination to combat smuggling, the Admiralty formed the Royal Navy Coast Blockade and entrusted its command to Captain James William McCulloch RN (known as Flogging Joey by his men).

An East Indiaman in full sail is an appropriate sign for this traditional maritime local.

McCulloch vowed to restore law and order in the town and make it such a peaceable place that grass would grow in its streets. Naturally the smugglers had other ideas. They were not prepared to relinquish their profitable way of life and confrontations intensified. Major affrays reached unprecedented savagery.

On one occasion Captain McCulloch detailed two midshipmen from the *Severn* to watch a pair of boatmen in Middle

The maritime feel of the pub is preserved with dark woodwork and pictures of local ships and shipwrecks.

Above left: There is a nice atmosphere in the evening with candles and a woodburner in the winter.

Above right: William Soames, Customs Searcher of Deal, was stabbed in the back by smugglers here in Middle Street in 1811.

Street who were suspected of handling contraband. One of the suspects, no doubt a regular at the Ship Inn, was recognized as the notorious scoundrel Will Worthington.

The two midshipmen gave chase and pursued the men through Middle Street to Lower Street and into the Fish Market where they were surrounded by a hostile crowd who had gathered in support of the smugglers. One of the midshipmen, James Taverner, panicked and fired a shot before diving for cover in a nearby shop. Taverner was promptly arrested by the corrupt Edward Iggulsden (who was both Mayor and magistrate) and committed for trial on a capital charge. Bail was refused.

On another occasion in 1818 William Soames, Customs Searcher of Deal, attempted to apprehend two boatmen who were strolling through Middle Street carrying a tub of spirits concealed in a sack. Soames gave chase and they dropped the sack but while he was examining it he was stabbed in the back with a large clasp knife.

Deal
The Royal Hotel

www.theroyalhotel.com royalhotel@shepherdneame.co.uk 01304 375555

The Royal was originally known as the King's Arms, but by 1699 the name had changed to the Three Kings. Today it is arguably Deal's classiest hotel but this wasn't always the case. In December 1801 Customs Officers captured a smuggling lugger near the Three Kings but as they were about to make off with their prize about 150 men stormed from the pub and retrieved the boat. A reward of £100 was offered for the apprehension of the men but it was never claimed.

Throughout the 1700s the pub was used as a courtroom where many a Deal boatman was tried for smuggling and for 'hovering'. The boatmen of Deal bought tea and other contraband from East Indiamen who hovered offshore in the sheltered area between the sandbanks called 'the Downs'. The shallow draft Deal Lugger could negotiate the treacherous

The Royal Hotel is the only building left remaining on the beach from the many that stood side by side until the 1830s.

Goodwin Sands where Revenue cutters and Navy blockade ships could not give chase. It was also possible for a crew to carry a galley across the Goodwin Sands at low tide making it totally impossible for any Revenue cutter to follow.

An interesting slant on Deal in the 1700s comes from the prominent Blue Stocking Elizabeth Carter who lived here from 1717 until 1806. She blamed the aristocratic customers – who should have known better – for buying the contraband: "I hear nothing here but tea and brandy, and prohibited clothing, which is bought up with a scandalous degree of eagerness by people of fashion and fortune."

Originally known as the Kings Arms, the Royal today is arguably Deal's classiest hotel.

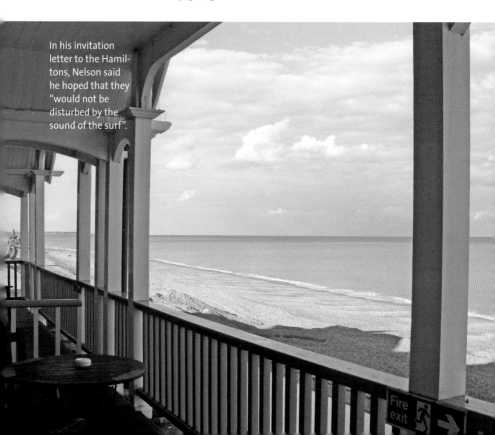

In his invitation letter to the Hamiltons, Nelson said he hoped that they "would not be disturbed by the sound of the surf".

Fire exit

OGDEN'S CIGARETTES

THE REVENUE CUTTER

The shallow draft Deal Lugger could negotiate the treacherous Goodwin Sands where Revenue cutters and navy blockade ships could not give chase.

Deal boatmen were both heroes and villains. Some of their sea rescues were of the most heroic order but they could also be looters and traitors. During the Napoleonic Wars they smuggled out spies, French prisoners of war, letters, newspapers and gold. It was at Deal that the 'Guinea boats' were constructed to ship the golden guineas to France to pay Napoleon's troops.

On the evening of 29 July, 1801 Lord Nelson arrived in Deal to take up his position of second-in-command of the Channel Fleet. He set up his shore headquarters in the Three Kings where he had a suite of three private rooms linked by a gallery overlooking the beach. He wrote to his friends Sir William and Lady Hamilton urging them to come to Deal, adding that: "The Three Kings, I am told is the best hotel. It stands on the beach... you can bathe in the sea which will make you strong and well... I hate the Downs but if my friends come it will be paradise."

In 1837 the Three Kings was re-furbished and re-opened under the name of the Royal Hotel in celebration of Queen Victoria's accession to the throne that year. The present day architecture suggests a build date of around 1720, replacing an earlier building, with the northern part added in the late Victorian era.

Displayed in the Deal Maritime Museum, the *Saxon King* is one of the two smuggling galleys that have miraculously survived.

The original building on this spot was erected in 1365 as accommodation for the Church-warden of neighbouring St James.

Dover
The White Horse
01304 213066

Charles Dickens, in *A Tale of two Cities*, described life in the Dover of the eighteenth-century: "A little fishing was done in the port, and a quantity of strolling about by night, and looking seaward: particularly at those times when the tide made, and was near flood. Small tradesmen, who did no business whatever, sometimes unaccountably realised large fortunes, and it was remarkable that nobody in the neighbourhood could endure a lamplighter."

Dickens was echoing an official Customs report of 1745 which stated there were an estimated 400 men involved in smuggling in Dover with no other obvious source of income. At that time Castle Hill was the main road from Dover to Deal and below the pub were saltpans – flat areas of sea-encroached land where sea water was evaporated to make salt. This is where smugglers' hoards were stashed; disguised under piles of sand and scrub.

Modern Dover has a scarcity of ancient buildings – including smugglers' pubs – because Hitler did his best to destroy them along with the rest of this ancient cinque port. The White Horse miraculously survived. St James church, which stood next door, did not; it was destroyed by enemy shelling in 1942.

Above left: The present pub dining room was used as a mortuary and inquests were held here mainly for people whose bodies had been washed up from the sea.

Above right: In the centre of the present interior there are a pair of 'exterior' doors, courtyard flagstones and a cellar entrance opening out of the carpeted floor.

In 2010 the pub was featured in a documentary about channel swimming. During the previous decade it had become a tradition for swimmers and their support teams to sign the walls and ceiling of the bar before and after their cross-channel swims.

Built in 1365, the pub was originally two cottages providing accommodation for the Churchwarden of St James. With the Dissolution of the Monasteries in 1539, the church gave up the property. From 1574, for the next 55 years, Dover's 'ale tasters' lived here. Their duties included checking on the quality of ale and on unlawful measures.

Somewhere around 1600 William Smith bought the building and converted it into an inn. And in 1635 Nicholas Ramsey was granted permission to call the premises the 'City of Edinburgh', after a ship that sank in the Dover Straits. The pub traded for something like 200 years after that before becoming The White Horse Inn.

The fate of the infamous Aldington Gang was finally sealed here in Dover at about one o'clock on 30 July 1826. They were caught unloading tubs on to the beach and, in the affray, Midshipman Quartermaster Richard Morgan from H.M.S. *Ramilies* was killed and Seaman Michael Picket was wounded.

A reward equivalent to ten years pay for a farm labourer was offered for information leading to arrests. Subsequently George Ransley and eighteen of his men were apprehended and tried for "being present, aiding, assisting and computing in the commission of murder". They were all sentenced to death but the sentences were commuted and they were instead transported to Tasmania.

The White Horse today is full of character with a number of softly lit interesting rooms on different levels. It retains the original cottagey feel with curtains and nick-nacks and pastel colours. There's lots of match boarding and exposed areas of stone and brick on the walls, as well as a homely mix of old furniture standing on carpeted areas or old pine floor boards.

Opposite: The fate of the infamous Aldington Gang was finally sealed here on Dover Beach at about one o'clock on 30 July 1826.

Below: Midshipman Quartermaster Richard Morgan from the 74 gun ship H.M.S. *Ramilies* was killed and Seaman Michael Picket was wounded.

OGDEN'S CIGARETTES

H.M.S. "RAMILLIES"

Hythe
The Bell
01303 267175

Located at the east end of the town, The Bell is believed to be the oldest pub in Hythe and would have been the harbour pub when the town was a flourishing port. The original deeds to the building were lost in the days when the inn was owned by the Mackeson Family, who ran the brewery in Hythe. Records of the inn that remain go back over four hundred years.

The Bell was a seafront tavern in medieval times where the chimney stack was used as a look-out point accessed by steps carved inside.

Much of the timber in this fine weatherboarded inn would have come from ships wrecked off the Romney Marsh at a time when this site was virtually on the water's edge. Hythe's harbour was eventually closed by the build-up of shingle, and pub and town were left high and dry.

The restaurant is named after the stream that flows under the building where contraband was concealed and floated through.

A comfortably upholstered corner of the old tavern still retains its bare board flooring.

During the late 1700s most of Hythe's inhabitants were involved in the lucrative smuggling trade and traces of those turbulent times can be found at The Bell including a tunnel close to an underground mill stream which runs under the pub. Here casks of gin and brandy were stored out of harm's way, being moved when required by a hoist connected to a hook in the attic, which has survived. Another convenient hiding place were the ledges on either side of the tunnelled drain through which the mill stream flowed.

One of the two back-to-back inglenooks where, in 1963, the gruesome discovery of the skeletons of two Revenue men was made.

There is a gap of a barrel's width between the back to back fireplaces which now divide the bar and restaurant. This was a quick and convenient internal route to move smuggled goods from the cellar to the rooms upstairs. The chimney stack (seen in the picture) was also used as a lookout point. Footholds are carved into the stone and the view from the top would have given smugglers a chance to hook up barrels if the authorities were approaching. A former landlord climbed the chimney and found a clay pipe, perhaps belonging to a smuggler who enjoyed a smoke when it was his watch.

In 1963, builder Colin Lepper, a regular at the pub made a gruesome discovery of two skeletons when he uncovered the back of the old inglenook fireplace. They were identified as being Revenue officers because their boots, belts, hats and badges had survived. All were taken to the local coroners except a couple of finger bones which were displayed in the bar for years as unusual souvenirs of the pub's history.

Today The Bell offers traditional ales; good food, comfort and more history than you could shake a sabre at. This is a smugglers' pub par excellence.

ROMNEY MARSH & ENVIRONS

Mersham
Farriers Arms
www.thefarriersarms.com 01233 720444

James Byham Ransley, father of the 'rascally brothers' James and William, quit Ruckinge with his family in 1792 and moved here to Mersham. The reason was possibly to be near the Hythe to Ashford turnpike. This afforded potential for highway robbery; as well as for moving smuggled goods from the Romney Marsh up to London. The three Ransley girls, Anne, Mary and Elizabeth also learned to rob travellers on the high road.

Jane Austen's brother Edward was a victim of James and William Ransley.

Among the catalogue of their crimes at this time, father and son James were jointly charged in 1799 with armed robbery and of "stealing eight bushels of pease... and one gallon of wheat" from Jane Austen's brother, Edward Austen Knight Esquire of Godmersham Park. Although it doesn't excuse the Ransley's crime, there can hardly have been a greater example

This wonderful former farmhouse was built in the third year of the reign of Elizabeth I.

of the haves and have-nots. Edward had inherited two great estates – each with its own mansion. He wore breeches and matching frock coats made of silk.

At the time the Ransleys moved to Mersham, John Epps and his son (also named John) owned the pub and the adjoining farrier's business. The premises may have been referred to then as the 'Blacksmith's Arms'. Father and son were both known to have taken part in the brewing of ales, and at that time were probably unlicensed. Epps senior worked the forge until 1802 when his son took over the business.

In April 1806 John Epps Junior married Mary Ransley. Her rascally brothers had been hanged six years earlier at Maidstone for highway robbery. Twenty years later, there was still a connection between the pub and the Ransleys. Thomas Wheeler had possessed the property before the Epps and, in 1826 his son Thomas Junior, was convicted of smuggling and

Inside is everything you would expect – beams, brickwork, boards, brass and beer.

deported to Tasmania, along with other members of the Ransley Gang including George, who was Mary's cousin and leader of the ruffians at that time.

Above left: The Farriers Arms is once again a thriving pub.

Built in the third year of the reign of Elizabeth I, this wonderful old building was initially a farm house forming part of the estate of one Simon Tindle. In 1632, whilst still in the hands of Tindle, the blacksmith's forge and stables were built. In 1828, John Epps Junior sold the house and forge to William Prebble, a farrier and common beer seller who, in 1829, was granted a licence to sell ales and ciders from a premises which he named the 'Farriers Arms'.

Above right: Head brewer Richard Dixey (seen on right) with some of the other Farriers Arms shareholders.

Below: The Ransley's square brick cottage still stands at the far end of Kingsford Street.

In 2009 the pub was about to close when 121 locals embarked on a plan to save it. They each bought a share in the pub and between them they helped stump up £430,000 for the purchase of the building and an additional £200,000 to pay for the renovation. They have now installed their own micro brewery on the premises where they produce the popular 'Farriers 1606' Kentish Country Ale.

Aldington
Walnut Tree Inn

www.walnuttreealdington.co.uk/index.html karen@walnuttree.com

01233 720298

The scattered village of Aldington stands on high ground overlooking the flat expanse of Romney Marsh. It would be unremarkable but for its association with the fearsome gang of smugglers known as the 'Aldington Blues'. During the early 1800s the gang operated openly and freely throughout East Kent. Aldington became their stronghold and the Walnut Tree their strategic headquarters.

The first leader of the Blues was Cephas Quested who, along with Richard Wraight, brother of the landlord of the Walnut Tree was finally captured at the 'Battle of Brookland' in 1821. Another member of the gang was wounded but made it back to the Walnut Tree and hid here successfully. Wraight was acquitted but Quested was hanged and the smugglers were left without a leader.

George Ransley took over as leader. Born at Ruckinge in 1782, he spent his early life blamelessly as a carter and ploughman. It is said that soon after his marriage he found a cache of spirits, and raised enough money from its sale to build his own house still known as the Bourne Tap. He ran this as a 'blind pig' – an unlicensed drinking den.

On 30 July 1826 he and his gang were involved in an affray at Dover when Midshipman Quartermaster Richard Morgan was killed and Seaman Michael Picket was wounded. Ten weeks later, acting on information received, Bow Street Runners and Blockade Officers arrived at Aldington at 3 a.m. and surprised the gang leaders in their beds. Eighteen of them were duly tried, and death sentences passed which were commuted to transportation for life to Tasmania. George Ransley was eventually pardoned, became a free settler himself, and ended his days there with the rest of his large family.

Dating back to the fourteenth century, the pub started life as a simple hall house and the people who farmed 10 acres that went with the property made their own cider and brewed their own beer. In the mid fifteenth century a small bedroom was added at a higher level accessed by a ladder. A light set in the window could be seen as far away as the Channel coast, to provide a warning or an all clear.

This small window, high up on the southern side of the inn, is where the gang would shine a signal light to their confederates on Aldington Knoll.

The Walnut Tree still looks the part and is full of nooks and crannies and confusing passages.

In the mid fifteenth century a small bedroom (top right) was added at a higher level. Accessed by a ladder, it was used by smugglers as a lookout and signalling post.

The nearby Bourne Tap is the house George Ransley built from ill-gotten gains and ran as an illegal drinking den.

In 1704, the property was purchased by Jonas Quilter who was granted a licence to sell ales and ciders. In 1749 it was owned by Thomas Gadhew, who registered the title 'Walnut Tree'.

The pub still looks the part today; its small leaded windows and sturdy doors a match for any Excise man. Inside it is full of nooks and crannies and confusing passages. The sign depicts an Excise man, sabre in hand, coming across two smugglers at night trying to hide under a tree with their contraband.

Steve and Karen, landlords of the Walnut Tree, are extremely knowledgeable and enthusiastic about the smuggling history of the pub.

Woodchurch
Bonny Cravat

www.shepherdneame.co.uk/pubs/ashford/bonny-cravat 01233 860345

Diamond House in Brook Street, Woodchurch is a 'British Listed Building'. English Heritage describes it as a four-bay hall house, possibly of late fourteenth century. Following the usual detailed list of architectural features they add this caveat: "The house was occupied by the Diamond Family, a notorious family of smugglers, from the late seventeenth century to 1748, and several alcoves reputed to be smugglers hides have been found in the house."

The brewery have settled on the theory that the name derives from 'a bonne corvette' or good ship.

During the 1740s smuggling in Kent had reached huge proportions and was heavily tainted with violence. In October 1747 the Hawkhurst Gang became involved in the audacious raid on Poole Customs House in Dorset. Among their number that day was John (Jack) Diamond. This incident ultimately led to the most brutal event in smuggling history with the torture and death of potential informer Daniel Chater and his chaperone, Customs Officer William Galley.

Woodchurch is a two pub village and they stand next to each other just up from the village green.

Above left: The popular dining room overlooks the church and the quiet village street.

Above right: For ten years from 1690 John Medhurst was the landlord who kept order and dispensed his beer direct from wooden barrels.

Events began when a Dorset gang of smugglers suffered the loss of a boat carrying two tons of tea and thirty-nine casks of spirit from Guernsey. The confiscated goods were sent to the Customs House at Poole and the Dorset smugglers sought the assistance of the Hawkhurst men to retrieve it.

The raid was successful and, on their way back to Kent, the men from Hawkhurst crossed the Avon at Fordingbridge in Hampshire. At the riverside George Inn, they rested their horses, took refreshment and divided the spoils. By the time they left, large numbers of people had gathered in the streets to cheer them on their way. One of the townsfolk, shoemaker Daniel Chater, recognized Diamond and called out to him by name. The former acquaintances had a laugh and joke and the smuggler threw the old man a bag of tea. The Collector of Customs for Southampton got to hear of the incident and summoned Chater to give evidence.

Chater never made it to court, nor did Crown witness William Galley, the Customs Officer who had taken his statement and provided his escort. They were both tortured and murdered in a manner that showed a depth of sadism, bestiality and brutality that shocked the whole nation. The smugglers had overstepped the mark and forfeited public tolerance. Other witnesses were found who would testify against them and the ringleaders were all hanged. There is no mention of the fate of John Diamond or reference to the family of that name in Woodchurch after that time.

Some say the unusual name of this pub was an ironic reference to the hangman's noose. There could be something in it, as the pub was often used as a courtroom and many times men received the death sentence here for sheep stealing. Another theory about the unique name is that it came from a French ship. This seems to be the explanation accepted by the brewery, as the pub sign depicts a 'Corvette', an eighteenth-century warship in full sail.

Throughout the turbulent period the Diamonds were drinking in this pub it was in the hands of the Fullager family.

Today the Bonny Cravat is a busy village pub with a popular restaurant and a very large garden; a particular favourite with families. The building is steeped in history and I think the stories of a former priesthole in the cellar and a tunnel leading directly to the church opposite (believed to date from the time of the Reformation) could well be true.

One of a number of alcoves in Diamond House reputed to be smugglers' hides.

Diamond House in Brook Street was occupied by the notorious family of smugglers, from the late seventeenth century to 1748.

Woodchurch
Six Bells

www.6-bells.co.uk info@6-bells.co.uk 01233 860246

Following the battle of Brookland in February 1821, and Cephas Quested's execution, George Ransley took over as leader of the last of the big smuggling gangs known as 'The Blues'. Ransley and other ring leaders of the North Kent Gang lived in the village of Aldington, but many of the foot soldiers, including Ransley family members, lived here in Woodchurch.

A big wisteria, which flowers in the spring and again in the summer, drapes the front of this exceedingly inviting pub.

In May 1826, a Blockade man was killed at Camber when two hundred smugglers from the North Kent Gang clashed with Preventative forces. A few days afterwards a party of Dragoons arrived in Woodchurch looking for contraband and for those involved in the fracas. A battle took place on the village green and two of the smugglers arrested were later to turn King's Evidence.

The fate of the gang was finally sealed in the July when they were caught unloading tubs onto the beach at Dover when Midshipman Richard Morgan from H.M.S. *Ramillies* was fatally wounded. A £500 reward was offered for information but no one came forward to claim it. Eventually, the two other gang members who had been captured in the earlier fighting provided the necessary intelligence.

In October 1826, acting on information received, eight men including the leader George Ransley, were arrested in a dawn raid on Aldington. By the end of the year, eleven more of the gang had been taken. At Maidstone Assizes on Friday 12 January 1827 death sentences were pronounced on all of them. The royal prerogative of mercy was exercised and punishment commuted to transportation for life. They were all dispatched to Tasmania.

Ransley's lived in Woodchurch cottages for nearly three centuries from the time parish records began.

Within a few years the names of Ransley family members who remained in Woodchurch were appearing on the Pauper List. And the name Ransley continued to appear regularly in parish records of births, deaths and marriages for nearly 300 years. The first recorded marriage took place on 3 June 1703

The church, which stands across the road from the pub, has a peal of six bells, with its tenor bell weighing in at three-quarters of a ton.

The Six Bells has a separate public bar and a saloon bar with a dining area, so there is plenty of bar area for drinkers.

Above left: The middle part of the house is old, with varying ceiling heights and a pleasing confusion of exposed beams.

Above right: With Shepherd Neame's presence only a stone's throw away the Six Bells remains fiercely free.

On certain summer Sunday afternoons a battle takes place here on the large green near the pub, but today the opposing sides stop for tea half way through.

between John Ransley and Dorothy Maxted. The last recorded was on 22 May 1976 when Stephen Thomas Ransley married his bride Angela Margaret Kirk.

The exceedingly inviting Six Bells is one door nearer the village green than the Bonny Cravat. A big wisteria, which flowers in the spring and again in the summer, drapes the front. And there are benches and tables in the garden from which to enjoy it.

The middle part of the house is old, with varying ceiling heights and a pleasing confusion of exposed beams. Not surprisingly, below the pub are some concealed cellars not easy for a revenue man to spot. The Six Bells has a separate public bar plus a saloon bar with a dining area, so there is plenty of bar area for drinkers.

Warehorne
The Woolpack Inn

www.thewoolpackwarehorne.co.uk 01233 733888

In the early days of its existence in England, smuggling took the form of illegal exportation rather than importation and was directly concerned with the wool trade, England's major industry during the medieval era. The Romney Marsh was the main centre for this illegal activity and the men involved were known as 'owlers' because they worked stealthily by night. The inn sign of The Woolpack Inn at Warehorne shows a couple of these characters at work with their pony and lantern.

By the Georgian period the emphasis, driven by heavy taxation, had shifted to the illegal importation of luxury goods, mainly spirits, tobacco and tea. The Woolpack Inn at Warehorne has the greatest physical evidence of smuggling that I have found in any pub. Inside a cupboard in the hall is the blocked up entrance to a tunnel which led directly to St Matthew's churchyard opposite. The tunnel emerges in the

The inn sign shows a couple of smugglers going about their stealthy work.

This neatly kept sixteenth-century pub restaurant is located in a lovely spot on a quiet lane near the Royal Military Canal.

Above left: The stone tower of St Matthew's church (opposite the pub) was struck by lightning in 1770 and, for economy, was rebuilt in brick.

Above right: A tombstone in the churchyard tilts to reveal the exit of the smugglers' tunnel.

graveyard on the far side of the church under a cleverly constructed fake grave mound. The headstone is moveable and tilts back to reveal the tunnel exit. English Heritage attests to the authenticity of the tunnel.

In 1817 R. H. Barham (author of the *Ingoldsby Legends*) was ordained and received the living at nearby Snargate and, at the same time, became the curate of Warehorne. Barham famously called the Marsh the 'Fifth Continent' because he found it to be a world unto itself. He elected to live in Warehorne Parsonage with his wife Caroline whom he had married in 1814.

Inside there is a comfortable rambling bar and spacious candlelit restaurant.

Barham reported that the rustic remoteness of Warehorne was a considerable advantage to "desperadoes engaged in what, by a technical euphemism, was termed – The Free Trade". Naturally he learned to turn a blind-eye to the smuggling activities of his parishioners. The tacit compliment was returned by the smugglers; "notwithstanding the reckless character of these men, I met with nothing of outrage or incivility at their hands."

Inside a hall cupboard is the blocked up entrance to a smugglers' tunnel.

Many a time, on returning homewards late at night, he was challenged by a half-seen horseman who looked in the heavy gloom like some misty condensation a little more substantial than ordinary fog. However on making known his name and office, he was invariably allowed to pass on with a "Good night, it's only parson!," while a long and shadowy line of mounted smugglers, each with his led horse laden with tubs, filed silently by.

Wool smugglers were known as 'owlers' because they worked stealthily by night.

Barham wrote his *Ingoldsby Legends* under the pseudonym, Thomas Ingoldsby, and included the story of Exciseman Gill who sold his soul for a demon horse that had the ability to catch Smuggler Bill. Though it sounds unlikely, it is a rewarding read.

OGDEN'S CIGARETTES

THE OWLERS

This neatly kept sixteenth-century pub restaurant started life as a farmhouse. It is located in a lovely spot on a quiet lane near the Royal Military Canal. Picnic sets among flower tubs overlook a meadow with beech trees. Inside there is a rambling bar with heavy beams, an inglenook and a woodburner. There is modern pine furniture in the spacious candlelit restaurant which is snug with sofas and armchairs.

The Red Lion at Snargate is not just unspoilt; it has remained virtually unaltered for over a century.

Snargate
Red Lion

01797 344648

The wonderful Doris Jemison standing by the unusual free-standing marble-topped counter in the candle-lit front bar.

The Red Lion at Snargate is not just unspoilt; it has remained virtually unaltered for over a century. This is because for nearly all that time it has been in the hands of one family. Doris Jemison is the current representative and, apart from opening up a private room to provide a little more space, she has not altered anything of consequence since her family took over in 1911.

Snargate is a remote hamlet on the western side of the Romney Marsh. It gets its name from the 'snare-gate' or sluice-gate

Traditional pub games in the back bar include 'table skittles' and 'toad in the hole' which consists of pitching brass discs into the top of the commode-like piece of furniture and ringing the bell inside.

systems used to defend the low-lying land reclaimed from the sea. The pub has been established for 450 years in this deep smuggling country. R. H. Barham (author of the *Ingoldsby Legends*) knew it well. He was Rector here from 1817 when the parish held 15 dwellings and a total population of 93 people. The parish church, a couple of hundred yards down the lane opposite, is dedicated to St Dunstan, and stands on a man-made mound, surrounded by trees.

The only way Barham, as an outsider, could function in this remote, tight-knit community was to turn a blind eye to the nocturnal illicit activities of the Snargate smugglers. He couldn't ignore them because of the large cargoes of contra-band tobacco stored in the church tower. This had such a pervasive odour he was able to locate the church by smell alone when travelling through the marsh mists.

Opposite the main door, on the north wall of St Dunstan's is a faint terracotta coloured painting of a ship of around the year 1500, which was discovered under a layer of whitewash. There was a tradition on the marshes that this was an owler's coded symbol marking a place of safety.

The Red Lion is definitely not a dining pub and if Doris Jemison has her way it never will be. It has a simple old-fash-ioned charm in three timeless little rooms with original cream

Above right: Nothing of consequence has been altered since the Jemison family took over in 1911.

Above left: Not everything is nostalgia. The piece of sheet music on the old piano is 'Say You, Say Me' by Lionel Richie and Doris was proud to show me the visi-tors' book signed by Paul and Linda McCartney.

Above left: The tower of St Dunstan's church served as a contraband warehouse.

Above right: The 500 year-old wall painting of the ship on the north wall of the church was an owler's coded symbol marking a place of safety.

wall panelling, coal fire and heavy beams in sagging ceilings. Dark pine Victorian farmhouse chairs stand on bare boards and there is an old piano stacked with books.

Local cider and four or five ales including Goachers are tapped from casks behind the unusual free-standing marble-topped counter. In the back bar there are traditional games like 'toad in the hole', 'nine men's morris' and 'table skittles'. Children are allowed in the family room, dogs in the bar and the lavatories are outside in the cottage garden.

The Romney or the Kent sheep is a 'longwool' sheep whose dense fleece was highly prized, leading to widespread wool smuggling.

The original yeoman's house adjoins the back of the Georgian pub.

Ruckinge
The Blue Anchor

www.blueanchorruckinge.com info@blueanchorruckinge.com
01233 732387

William Ireland, in his *History of Kent* gives us a picture of Ruckinge in 1829: "The village is obscure, little known, extremely dreary and unpleasant, the soil is deep and miry clay, the parish for the most part inhabited by poor people."

These poor people were of course mainly farm labourers who were soon to riot for 2/6d (12p) daily pay. They were naturally only too willing to supplement a meagre income by carrying illicit cargo inland for the smugglers and earning in one night the equivalent of a fortnight's wages from honest toil.

Highway robbery and a graveboard are depicted on the village sign.

The inn was built in 1738 as a farm dwelling with 6 acres. Ezra Ballard, a farmer and grazier of Bilsington was granted an ale licence here in 1765. Ten years later it had come to be known as the 'Blue Anchor Ale House'. After Ezra's death in 1779 his wife Naomi continued to run the pub until her death when

Today the interior is open plan with lounge, bar and restaurant.

A see through fire place effectively divides the room spaces.

her son Isaac took over. As we shall see later, Isaac Ballard, was to add his name to the annals of Ruckinge's criminal history.

By 1788 when James Wilson, grazier and beer seller became the owner, the pub had been altered and extended. He was granted a full licence and the house began trading as the 'Blue Anchor Inn'. Eleven years later, in the April of 1799, an argument broke out in the pub during which James's wife Anne was assaulted. William Ransley was convicted of the attack and was sentenced to three months hard labour which he served in Canterbury Gaol.

On Thursday 24 August 1800, just a year after his release, William was publicly hanged on Peneden Heath, Maidstone along with his brother James for the crime of armed burglary. On the same day, Isaac Ballard, the one time keeper of The Blue Anchor, was also hanged for highway robbery; John Parsons for sheep stealing and Robert Radford for rape which took place outside The Blue Anchor Inn.

The Ransley's curiously shaped cottage suggests they were never able to afford to add a second storey.

By that time James Byham Ransley had moved with his family to Mersham but it was their right to be buried in their home parish of Ruckinge. James senior travelled to Maidstone with a cart to collect the corpses of his sons to convey them to their last and final resting place.

In Ruckinge village churchyard, a hefty grave-board marks the spot where various members of the villainous Ransley family lie buried. These included James Byham Ransley and his sons James and William, still known locally as 'the rascally brothers'. Today a graveboard is a comparative rarity but, in years gone by, it was a common enough marker for those who were unable to afford the more durable gravestone.

The roadside church of St Mary Magdalene is worth a visit to see the two splendid Norman doorways.

The names and dates on the grave-board have long since been bleached by two centuries of hot summer suns and biting marsh winters.

Dymchurch,
The Ship Inn
www.shipinn.biz info@shipinn.biz 01303 872122

For six-hundred years The Ship Inn has stood defiant against the elements by the sea wall at Dymchurch. Today the road passes behind the old inn and the first thing you see journeying south is the faithful reproduction of a gibbet hanging from a tree in the garden. Inside the pub is a history of this gruesome piece of apparatus used to display the rotting corpses of executed felons. It was designed to act as a warning and deterrent to other would be smugglers, wreckers and sheep stealers.

In the 1900s, author Russell Thorndike, brother of the famous actress Dame Sybil, was a resident of Dymchurch. Stories of local 'free traders' captured his imagination and he wrote a series of seven novels centred on The Ship Inn where he was a regular. The pub had been a smugglers' haunt in real life and also played host to the local coroner's court, where

Today the road passes to the rear of the sixteenth-century inn.

In the pub garden there is faithful replica of a gibbet complete with gibbet irons swinging from the beam.

Below left:
A panel in the entrance hall drops down to reveal a smugglers' hiding place in a cavity between the walls.

Below right:
A separate dining room and bar lead off from the entrance lobby.

There is a light modern feel to the dining room.

inquests were held into the deaths of many smugglers and fishermen lost at sea.

Thorndike's fictional hero, the Reverend Doctor Christopher Syn, was the respectable vicar of Dymchurch by day; who became 'the Scarecrow' – feared leader of the 'Marsh Men' gang of smugglers by night. Thorndike had his Jekyll and Hyde preacher delivering sermons in the church of St Peter and St Paul (across the road from the pub), which has a brass plaque commemorating the author. Many gravestones and tombs in the churchyard provided inspiration for the names of his characters.

The Syn stories were several times made into films and stills and posters from these decorate the bar. The most notable is the Disney version starring Patrick McGoohan. There is even a 'Scarecrow Ale' on tap, brewed by the Wychwood Brewery Company. Dymchurch village celebrates its connection to Russell Thorndike and his stories by staging a 'Day of Syn' on a biennial basis usually held during the August Bank Holiday weekend. Re-enactments of various parts of the books can be seen at many locations throughout the village, with the 'Kings Men', 'Mr Mipps' the Sexton coffin maker and, of course, 'The Scarecrow' in attendance – it is great fun.

The bar is decorated with stills and posters from films made of the Dr Syn stories.

Brookland
The Royal Oak
royal-oak-brookland.co.uk 01797 344025

It is hard to believe today that the pretty, peaceful village of Brookland, situated between the Walland and Romney Marshes, was once the scene of one of the major battles of the smuggling era. In the 1820s smuggling in east Kent was dominated by the activities of the Aldington Gang who operated along the stretch of coast between Deal and Rye under the leadership of the splendidly named Cephas Quested.

This present day civilised pub became a temporary mortuary and field hospital at the time of the 'Battle of Brookland'. From 1570 until 1736 it was a clergy house for St Augustine's; one of only four churches in England with a separate bell tower.

Quested was an accomplished organizer who could muster hundreds of labourers from a broad area to assist in unloading a cargo. A typical run would involve up to twenty oarsmen rowing one of the long, light, galleys across from France loaded with tobacco, spirits and salt. A high speed crossing of the Channel at night could be accomplished in five hours if the tide was favourable.

The large windows provide a light airy feel to the bar area.

The beamed restaurant has well spaced tables and a big inglenook.

On arrival, there would be a land party of two hundred or so. These comprised the customary corridor of armed men protecting the others who unloaded and moved the contraband quickly on shore and inland. On 11 February 1820, at around two thirty in the morning, just such a run was taking place at Camber Sands when the smugglers were spotted by a blockade patrol.

OGDEN'S CIGARETTES

THE " BATMAN "

Within a short time a running battle began, as the smugglers retreated across Walland Marsh towards Brookland, firing repeatedly as they went. The prolonged confrontation was bloody and bitter culminating in the arrest of Cephas Quested and Joseph Wraight. They were tried at the Old Bailey on 11 April 1821. The most damning piece of evidence against Quested, which sealed his fate on the gallows, was that in the thick of the battle, he mistook a blockade man for a smuggler and handed him a pistol, suggesting that the man should "blow an officer's brains out". On 4 July 1821, at the age of just 33, Quested was hanged at Newgate Prison.

During the year before the battle, The Royal Oak was trading as a beer house and leased to Johnathan Grist who applied for and was granted a wine and spirit licence. On the night of the fracas, Grist and his family were wakened by the noise of intense fighting in which four smugglers were killed and sixteen wounded. Midshipman McKenzie lay dead and eight other blockade men were wounded. The pub became a temporary mortuary and field hospital.

The customary corridor of armed men protected the others who unloaded and moved the contraband quickly on shore and inland.

Ralph Pepworth Hougham, the village surgeon, lived here at Pear Tree House, a few yards along the village street from the pub.

Brookland village surgeon, Ralph Pepworth Hougham, lived at Pear Tree House a few yards along the village street from the pub. He was often called out to treat wounded from both sides in these encounters but he would be led blindfolded on horseback by the smugglers to prevent him giving them away or being asked to appear in court and give evidence on oath.

The Royal Oak, which today is a haven of civilization, began life as a house in 1570. A succession of parish clerks and sextons lived here until 1736 when it became a pub. Sensitive restoration has ensured that the sixteenth-century building has retained its attractive timeless feel.

Large windows light the bar area and the spacious beamed restaurant with its big inglenook. A well kept tranquil garden borders the churchyard of St Augustine's, one of only four churches in England with a separate bell tower.

Brookland
The Woolpack Inn

www.shepherdneame.co.uk/pubs/romney-marsh/woolpack-inn
01797 344321

When smuggling was rife on the Romney Marsh the isolated location of this old treasure of a tavern, hidden down a deep lane a mile out of the village, was ideal for the clandestine activities of the owlers and free traders. Today, in common with other remote rural pubs, attracting visitors is a priority. To this end, the roof here is used as a giant advertising hoarding. 10 feet high white letters painted on the old red-brown Kent Peg tiles proclaim: 'WOOLPACK 15TH CENTURY INN'.

The fertile reclaimed land of the marsh made fine grazing for hundreds of thousands of sheep, and the export of wool from

This ancient inn dates from 1410 and was originally a beacon keeper's cottage.

The roof of The Woolpack holds out a promise to passing travellers.

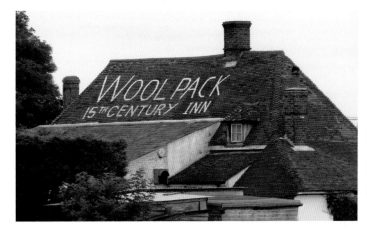

The simple bar with its massive inglenook. The two pub cats, Charlie Girl (seen here on the left) and Liquorice, vie with each other to demonstrate the fact that the inglenook is large enough to sit in.

their backs was for centuries both highly taxed and badly policed – almost an open invitation to smuggle. Illegal wool exports from the marsh probably started on the day restrictions were imposed in 1275 when the government introduced a tax of £3 a bag on wool leaving England.

By 1700 up to 150,000 'packs' of wool a year were being shipped from the area days after shearing. From these beginnings the Huguenot families who controlled the trade grew into the first smuggling gangs. In 1660 wool exports were forbidden, and two years later the death penalty was introduced for smuggling. The legislators of the day probably saw this as a major deterrent, but if anything, it simply made the owlers more desperate. If you're to hang for smuggling, why hesitate to shoot your pursuer in an attempt to evade capture?

Situated both historically and geographically in the birthplace of smuggling in Southern England, The Woolpack Inn dates from 1410 and was originally a beacon keepers cottage and the lane is known as Beacon Lane. It has been trading as a pub for over 400 years.

The spinning jenny mounted in the ceiling of the simple quarry tiled main bar, was used to divide up the smugglers' spoils.

The sign is a survival from the days when the 'woolstaplers' (wool graders) of the Weald passed this way with their laden packhorses.

The sunken tiled floor of the entrance worn by generations of marsh folk.

Very little had to be altered when Edwardian period scenes from 'The Loves of Joanna Godden', starring Googie Withers, were filmed here in 1947.

Low-beamed ceilings incorporate some very early ships' timbers; maybe from the twelfth century when the sea came right up to the meadow. The beams are all pegged; no nails except some formidable hand-made ones in the wattle and daub walls, some of these walls have been knocked down to merge all the original small rooms into one bar.

For centuries, thirsty traders would have entered the pub through the same ancient lobby you see today; with its uneven brick floor and black-painted pine-panelled walls. The Woolpack Inn is so perfectly authentic that very little had to be altered when scenes from the Edwardian sheep-farming saga 'The Loves of Joanna Godden' were filmed here in 1947.

Located in great walking country, this is a perfect place to stop and satisfy the thirst and appetite during a day out. The pub has two large beer gardens with neat lawns, shrubs, hanging baskets, plenty of picnic-sets under parasols and a barbecue area.

Lydd
George Hotel

www.thegeorgelydd.com tim@thegeorgelydd.com 01797 321710

In 1462 an ale house existed on the site of the George; almost certainly established to accommodate the masons who built the church. Cardinal Wolsey, who was rector here, raised the tower to 132 ft. high, and made the pinnacles a sign for every ship that passes down the channel.

The newly constructed George opened for business in 1620 and traded successfully as an inn for the next 243 years, when it became registered as a hotel. During this time, as a staging post for London Coaches, it became a meeting point for famous smuggling gangs, and was also used to keep prisoners before trial.

The church, the George Hotel and the adjoining red brick Town Hall, stand in the High Street which runs along what was once a shingle bank.

The most turbulent period of the inn's history occurred during the era of the Black-lock family. When Jacob Blacklock died in 1676, it passed to his son Jeremiah who was landlord here on 7 April 1694 when a gang of smugglers attacked and ransacked many of the rooms looking for clothier William Carter. Carter, who was staying here, had published a pamphlet on the evils of smuggling and had unsuccess-fully attempted to have six smugglers arrested.

OGDEN'S CIGARETTES

·THE FIGHT

In 1708 the inn passed from Jeremiah to his son Stanton who, in 1721, witnessed the biggest fracas. It became known as 'The Battle of Lydd' and took place in the inn. Jacob Walter and Thomas Bigg, smugglers from Mayfield, were taken as they came ashore from a French sloop at Dungeness. They were manacled, brought to the George and placed under armed guard. Land-lord Stanton Blacklock has left us with this eye witness account:

When appre-hended by the authorities smugglers did not hesitate to fight.

Opposite:
Top: On the wall in the bar are details of 550 years of the George's history.
Bottom left: In 1721, nine men ran up this staircase firing their pistols all the way.
Bottom right: The door at the end of this narrow hallway leads directly into the Town Hall.

"They was in a chamber, 6 officers with them, 20 firelocks loaded with powder and ball, at 5 o'clock on Sunday night 9 men well mounted and as well armed with pistols, swords, coopers adzes, wood bills and forks, comes up to ye house, dismounts from their horses and runs upstairs, firing all ye way. They wounded 3 officers and got between the officers and their arms and carried away Walter and Biggs; if these 9 men had not carried them off, a 100 more was hard by ready to make another attack. Jacob Walter was later recaptured by a commander in the Queens' Dragoons. The outcome of Thomas Biggs is unknown."

The confident little chap with the beard in the centre of this photograph looks remarkably like Joseph Conrad who lived on the Marsh and often visited Lydd.

A century later, William Fisher was the inn-keeper who played host to the Aldington Gang. In February 1821 Customs and Excise men had clashed with the gang at Brookland. Victims who died in the 'Battle of Brookland' and many other fights, are buried in All Saints churchyard.

Victims who died in the 'Battle of Brookland' and many other fights are buried in All Saints churchyard.

Lydd had been the most notorious of all the marsh smuggling centres; and it was here in 1829 townsfolk stood outside the George and cheered as a convoy of eighty men with twelve carts full of contraband passed through after the last major landing.

WEALD & HEARTLAND

Goudhurst
Star & Eagle Hotel

www.starandeagle.com   starandeagle@starandeagle.com   01580 211512

This superb fifteenth-century inn and the adjacent St Mary's church stand 400 ft. above sea level commanding views across Goudhurst and the Kentish Weald. In the spring of 1747 the inn and the church played a part in one of the most curious episodes of Kent's long smuggling history.

During the Battle of Goudhurst the militia commanded the high ground here by the church and inn.

In the attractive bar you are reminded of the days when the forests of the Weald provided England with the timber for her ships and for her homes.

The whole place is full of original features and provides a high level of comfort, style and character.

The Tudor dining room was formerly the kitchen.

The local Hawkhurst Gang who frequented the inn, had begun terrorizing the local community. Goudhurst citizens had become afraid to venture forth in the streets even in broad daylight. In April of that year, William Sturt, a soldier returned from the wars, found the villagers discussing evacuation. At this time the leader of the gang was a desperate rogue called Thomas Kingsmill, who had been raised in Goudhurst.

With a plot reminiscent of a Hollywood western, Sturt formed a local militia to protect the townsfolk against the outlaws. Word of this initiative soon got back to Kingsmill who flew into a violent rage declaring to kill all the villagers and burn every house to the ground. He even set the deadline of 21 April for a show-down.

Sturt had only formed the militia a short time before but he straightway set about giving them basic training. Trenches were dug, barricades were built, lead musket balls were made and two hundredweight of gunpowder obtained.

At the appointed time, and true to his word, Thomas Kingsmill arrived with his gang on the edge of the village shouting insults and violent threats at the defending force. William Sturt had delivered a stirring speech to his forces and they had positioned themselves on the high ground around the inn and even on the church tower. The scene was set. Kingsmill declared that in the evening he would dine off the hearts of four of the captured villagers.

Skull and Crossbones crown the headstone on the grave of George Kingsmill; brother of Thomas and early fatality at the Battle of Goudhurst.

The smugglers advanced but soon found that the few days of training and preparation by an experienced soldier was more than they had bargained for. Thomas Kingsmill's brother George, died from a bullet wound and at least two other smugglers were killed almost immediately in the rounds of musket fire that were exchanged. Several others were

Spyways in the High Street was a known smugglers' haunt.

wounded and at this point the smugglers' force was so weakened and demoralized they fled the scene with the villagers chasing them across the valley with their improvised weapons.

More smugglers were wounded and several were later apprehended, tried for their crimes and hanged. William Sturt became a local hero. In a western he would have been asked to take on the role of sheriff. Instead he was appointed Master of the Goudhurst Workhouse – with accommodation for himself and his family.

The inn was originally called the 'Black Spread Eagle' and the licence dates from 1600. Bedrooms and public rooms boast original features and great character. The cellars, where contraband would have been stored, are reminiscent of medieval dungeons. Massive vaulted stonework suggests this rambling, heavily beamed building may once have been a monastery and the tunnel from the cellars probably surfaces underneath the church.

Real Ale aficionados owe a debt to the Flemish weavers who settled in these cottages by the church around 1350. They preferred 'hopped' beer to English ale and they brought with them new varieties of hops and the knowledge of how to use them in brewing.

Built in the early 1400s the Oak & Ivy became a safe but seditious sanctuary for the biggest and most violent gang of smugglers this country has ever seen.

The Hawkhurst Community Partnership has established a 'Smugglers Trail' with a leaflet guide and porcelain plaques like this for the outside of the 20 participating establishments.

Hawkhurst
Oak & Ivy

www.theoakandivy.co.uk oakandivycontact@yahoo.com 01580 753293

The first part of this historic building was reputedly built in 1411. It consisted of just the right-hand side of the present pub. The steep pitch of the roof indicates that it would have been a thatched hall house. The inglenook fireplace has been dated to the late seventeenth century when the pub was extended to its present size.

The Civil War of the seventeenth-century inspired the pub's name. In a divided country public places needed to indicate where their loyalties lay. Pubs with 'Oak' in their name, particularly The Royal Oak, inclined towards support of the Royalists. Ivy was thought to kill mighty oak trees and so adding this to the name showed the pub welcomed a more parliamentary minded clientele.

A century after the war had finished the Oak & Ivy became a safe but seditious sanctuary for the 'Hawkhurst Gang' – the

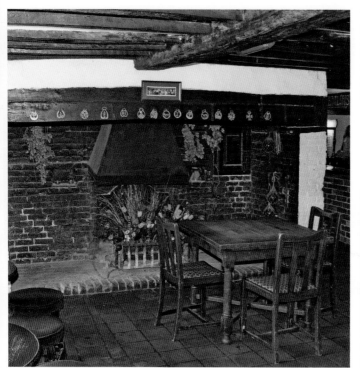

The inglenook fireplace has been dated to the late seventeenth-century when the pub was extended to its present size.

Paul Baxter, the current landlord is great fun and has a real interest in the pub's smuggling history.

Today the Oak & Ivy has the confident lively personality of a good all-round village local. It has the unmistak-able feel of a real pub – something to which people respond to instinctively.

Moosh the pub dog keeps a watchful eye out for the Excise men.

biggest and most violent gang of smugglers this country has ever seen. In the absence of really effective opposition smuggling grew to massive proportions.

The process was accelerated in the early years of the eighteenth century by widespread support for the Jacobite cause who took the ivy leaf as their emblem. Smuggling was seen not just as a business transaction, but also as an act of rebellion and support for the Old Pretender. Some of the smuggling gangs openly supported the Jacobites and drank their health.

These sympathies manifested themselves in more tangible ways, too. Jacobites travelled secretly between France and England on smuggling boats and some smugglers are known to have acted as spies and double agents for the cause.

The Hawkhurst Gang hatched their plans for smuggling contraband across from France and the Channel Islands at meetings held in this pub. Their haunt was well chosen for its position on the Rye Road to London within easy reach of onward staging posts.

Further up the London Road towards the village centre stands the imposing Queen Inn. Evidence of a tunnel has been found here in the cellars which is thought once linked the two pubs.

Wrotham
The Bull Hotel

www.thebullhotel.com info@thebullhotel.com 01732 789800

Located right on the Pilgrims Way, Wrotham has always had good communications with London and the Kent coast.

During the nineteenth century, a Wrotham family became experts in 'free trade' logistics. They had a legitimate transport business, carrying goods between Sandwich and London, which served as a splendid cover for an equally successful and even more lucrative smuggling enterprise.

One member of the family, who was born around 1800, became known to his associates as 'Old Sobers'. In later life he related his reminiscences to a City businessman called John Terry who arranged to have them published. Old Sobers obviously came from a prosperous family because he told Terry: "we could muster 50 horses". These together with those belonging to the men of Platt and Ightham could quickly be increased to a 200 strong force, large enough to resist trouble.

The six-hundred-year-old Bull is now a smart twenty-first-century country hotel. The comfortable lounge and bar area has a timeless feel.

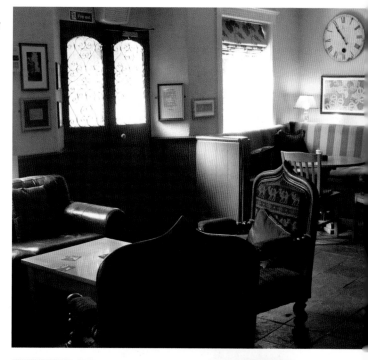

During WWII The Bull was frequented by fighter pilots from nearby Biggin Hill and the pub has many mementoes to the gallant few.

This early photograph shows that The Bull once enjoyed clear views across the countryside.

The family dealt in silks, lace, tobacco and spirits and had a city agent for each commodity. Old Sobers told how his father would change out of his working clothes and go in style by coach to Wood Street to meet his London merchant contacts. He also tells us how, at the age of thirteen, he would be sent at midnight in a pony trap called a 'dog cart' with a message for someone in 'the marsh'. At 17, he took a cart load of brooms to sell in London and returned next day with £1,000. In his early twenties he went to Flushing to become the family agent and buyer there.

In 1786, a few years before Old Sobers was born, Jeremiah Shadwell took over as keeper of the Bull, leasing it from Francis Gibbon, a brewer and maltster of Wateringbury. The new landlord stayed on for thirteen years through the height of the smuggling activity. At eight o'clock on the morning of the 1 June 1799 Jeremiah's brother, Lieutenant Colonel Peter Shadwell of the 25th Regt of Light Dragoons pulled up outside.

He had been travelling in a curricle from Lewisham with his servant John Self en route for Maidstone, where he was Commandant of the Cavalry Depot. Outside the pub he confronted a couple of men he thought might be deserters. After questioning them he tried to apprehend them and was shot dead.

Some sources say that the forty-seven-year-old Lieutenant Colonel was the gentleman leader of the local smuggling gang but I can find no evidence to support this. Traditionally Dragoons and smugglers were arch enemies and the incident

The wall tablet in the magnificent All Saints Church Maidstone pays tribute to a valuable officer and a sincere friend.

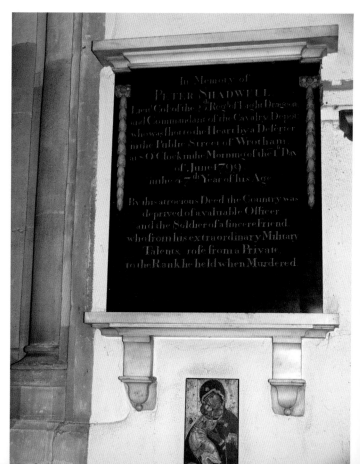

In Memory of
PETER SHADWELL
Lieut Col of the 25 Regt of Light Dragoon
and Commandant of the Cavalry Depot
who was Shot to the Heart by a Deserter
in the Public Street of Wrotham
at 8 O Clock in the Morning of the 1st Day
of June 1799
in the 47th Year of his Age

By this atrocious Deed the Country was
deprived of a valuable Officer
and the Soldier of a sincere Friend
who from his extraordinary Military
Talents, rose from a Private
to the Rank he held when Murdered

which took place outside the pub seems to suggest a devotion to duty. There is a memorial near the pub and another in All Saints church, Maidstone where he is buried.

The eulogy in the church reads: "By this atrocious Deed the Country was deprived of a valuable Officer and the soldier of a sincere Friend who from his extraordinary Military talents, rose from a Private to the Rank he held when Murdered". My theory is that Jeremiah Shadwell, the pub landlord, was the smuggler and that his brother Peter's name has been forever besmirched.

> Near this Place fell
> Lieu' Colonel SHADWELL.
> who was fhot to the Heart
> by a Deferter on the Morning
> of the Firft day of June 1709
> *The Afafsin with another*
> *Deferter his companion,*
> *were immediately fecured*
> *and brought to Juftice*

The plaque on the wall beside the pub marks the spot where Lieutenant Colonel Peter Shadwell was shot dead.

The inn first started trading under the sign of the Bull in 1385 during the reign of Richard II, and was first licensed under Henry VII in 1495. The rambling old coaching inn has recently undergone a labour of love refurbishment to emerge as a smart twenty-first- century country hotel.

The Vigo Inn on the summit of Wrotham Hill provided a signal point for local smugglers and a contraband storage depot. During building work a secret cupboard was discovered behind the tap room chimney.

These authentic gibbet irons, together with other real smuggling artifacts, are on display in Ypres Tower just over the Sussex border in Rye. The tower, now a museum, was formerly a prison where smugglers were frequently incarcerated.

THE SMUGGLERS

c. 1740, Dr Isaac Rutton (Seasalter, Blue Anchor)

Dr Rutton from Ashford was the founder member of the 'Seasalter Company'. This innocent sounding title was used to designate a number of ostensibly respectable individuals to conceal the nature of their smuggling activities.

d. 1748, Arthur Gray (Hawkhurst, Oak & Ivy)

Arthur Gray, one of the first leaders of the notorious Hawkhurst Gang was executed in 1748 for the murder of Thomas Carswell.

d. 1749 Thomas Kingsmill (Goudhurst, Star & Eagle)

In 1748, Thomas Kingsmill took over leadership of the Hawkhurst Gang following Arthur Gray's execution. Under his leadership the gang was defeated in a pitched battle by the Goudhurst Militia. Kingsmill was executed at Tyburn in 1749 following the raid on the Customs House in Poole and the grisly murders of William Galley and Daniel Chater.

d. 1750, Gabriel Tomkins (Hawkhurst, Oak & Ivy)

Tomkins led an extraordinary life. A bricklayer from Tunbridge Wells, he rode with the Hawkhurst Gang, led the Mayfield smugglers, became a customs officer, went back to smuggling, was shot, arrested, jailed, transported and finally hanged in Bedford for highway robbery.

1784, Richard Daws (Deal, King's Head)

Together with other Deal publicans who were involved in smuggling, Richard Daws witnessed the devastating event of boat burning on Deal beach on 15 January 1784.

d. 1800 James & William Ransley (Mersham, Farriers Arms)

Sons of James Byham Ransley and known as 'the rascally brothers' James and William were publicly hanged on Penenden Heath, Maidstone, on 20 August 1800 – the culmination of a joint career that embraced burglary, horse stealing, smuggling, highway robbery and common assault.

d. 1817 James Byham Ransley (Ruckinge, Blue Anchor)

Patriarch of the 'Roaring Ransleys', James Byham Ransley quit Ruckinge and moved with his family to Mersham in 1792 where he died aged 69 on Christmas Day.

d. 1821, Cephas Quested (Brookland, Royal Oak)

Quested, leader of the Aldington smuggling gang, was sentenced to death in 1821. He had been captured at the Battle of Brookland and accused of the murder of Midshipman McKenzie.

c. 1827 George Ransley (Aldington, Walnut Tree)
George took over leadership of the Aldington smuggling gang following Cephas Quested's death. He was transported to Tasmania with seven other members of the gang in January 1827.

d. 1837, Joss Snelling (Kingsgate, Captain Digby)
Snelling, known as 'The Broadstairs Smuggler' was born in St Peter's, Broadstairs in 1741 and, following a highly successful smuggling career, died peacefully in 1837.

d. 1890, 'Old Sobers' (Wrotham, Bull)
Son of the great smuggling family of Wrotham, Old Sobers was initiated into the wicked trade at an early age and left memoirs of his experiences.

George Ransley and seven members of the Aldington Gang were transported to Tasmania in 1827. This picture of a Government Jail Gang in Australia was published in London in 1830.

A Smuggler's Song
Rudyard Kipling

IF you wake at midnight, and hear a horse's feet,
Don't go drawing back the blind, or looking in the street,
Them that ask no questions isn't told a lie.
Watch the wall my darling while the Gentlemen go by.

Five and twenty ponies,
Trotting through the dark -
Brandy for the Parson, 'Baccy for the Clerk.
Laces for a lady; letters for a spy,
Watch the wall my darling while the Gentlemen go by!

Running round the woodlump if you chance to find
Little barrels, roped and tarred, all full of brandy-wine,
Don't you shout to come and look, nor use 'em for your play.
Put the brishwood back again - and they'll be gone next day!

If you see the stable-door setting open wide;
If you see a tired horse lying down inside;
If your mother mends a coat cut about and tore;
If the lining's wet and warm - don't you ask no more!

If you meet King George's men, dressed in blue and red,
You be careful what you say, and mindful what is said.
If they call you "pretty maid," and chuck you 'neath the chin,
Don't you tell where no one is, nor yet where no one's been!

Watch the wall my darling while the Gentlemen go by!

Knocks and footsteps round the house - whistles after dark -
You've no call for running out till the house-dogs bark.
Trusty's here, and Pincher's here, and see how dumb they lie
They don't fret to follow when the Gentlemen go by!

'If You do as you've been told, 'likely there's a chance,
You'll be give a dainty doll, all the way from France,
With a cap of Valenciennes, and a velvet hood -
A present from the Gentlemen, along 'o being good!

Five and twenty ponies,
Trotting through the dark -
Brandy for the Parson, 'Baccy for the Clerk.
Them that asks no questions isn't told a lie -
Watch the wall my darling while the Gentlemen go by!

BIBLIOGRAPHY

John Douch *Smuggling - The Wicked Trade*

Steve Glover & Michael Rogers
   The Old Pubs of Deal and Walmer

Stuart Harrison *Customs and Smugglers in the
   Port of Faversham*

Wallace Harvey *The Seasalter Company a Smuggling
   Fraternity*

Wallace Harvey *Whitstable and the French Prisoners of War*

Gregory Holyoake *Deal - Sad Smuggling Town*

Geoffrey Hufton & Elaine Baird *The Scarecrow's Legion*

Bridget Lely *Smuggling in Kent*

G. M. Rainbird *Inns of Kent*

Russell Thorndyke *Doctor Syn*

D. B. Tubbs *Kent Pubs*

Mary Waugh *Smuggling in Kent and Sussex*